Step by step,
the tell-tale trail of blood
was not hard to follow, and
it led from the corpses straight to the killers.

Before the week was out,
the guilty would hang,
while the crowd murmured prayers for the dead.

Life in Arizona Territory was a battle, and
death was often brutal and sudden,
without warning and — sometimes — without reason.

**RIDE THE TRAILS AND HOUND THE GUILTY
THROUGH 18 TRUE-LIFE ACCOUNTS OF**

MANHUNTS & MASSACRES

Read other books in the
WILD WEST COLLECTION,
fast-paced, true stories of when the Old West
was still young and rowdy, where anything
could happen — and too often did.

DAYS OF DESTINY

THEY LEFT THEIR MARK

THE LAW OF THE GUN

TOMBSTONE CHRONICLES

STALWART WOMEN

Coming Soon
INTO THE UNKNOWN

Design: MARY WINKELMAN VELGOS
Copy Editor: EVELYN HOWELL
Research: JEB STUART ROSEBROOK
Production: ELLEN STRAINE
Photographic enhancement: VICKY SNOW
Front cover art: *Holdup in the Canyon*, N.C. WYETH, Courtesy of Bank One.
Tooled leather design on covers: KEVIN KIBSEY AND RONDA JOHNSON-FREEMAN

AUTHORS:
Leo W. Banks, Chapters 1, 6, 7, 8, 9, 10, 13, 14, 15, 16, 17, and 18;
James E. Cook, Chapter 2; Sally Zanjani, Chapter 3; Susan Hazen-Hammond,
Chapter 4; Sam Negri, Chapter 5; Don Dedera, Chapter 12.

Prepared by the Book Division of *Arizona Highways*® magazine, a monthly
publication of the Arizona Department of Transportation.

Publisher — Nina M. La France
Managing Editor — Bob Albano
Associate Editor — Evelyn Howell
Art Director — Mary Winkelman Velgos
Production Director — Cindy Mackey

Printed in the United States
Library of Congress Catalog Number 96-80516
ISBN 0-916179-63-X

Manhunts & Massacres

Authors:

LEO W. BANKS
JAMES E. COOK
DON DEDERA
SUSAN HAZEN-HAMMOND
SAM NEGRI
SALLY ZANJANI

Book Editor:
ROBERT J. FARRELL

CONTENTS

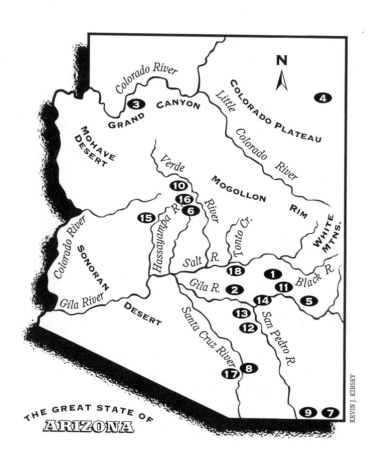

THE GREAT STATE OF ARIZONA

KEVIN J. KIBSEY

L E G E N D

1. Tuttle's Station
2. Apache Leap
3. Sharp Knife
4. Massacre Cave
5. Chacón
6. Goddard Station

7. Guadalupe Canyon
8. Hernandez Family
9. Lucero
10. Parker
11. Wham Robbery
12. Power Brothers

13. Gun Battle
14. Riverside Stage
15. Stanton
16. Townsend
17. Leatherwood
18. Woolsey

POSSE OF NAVAJO COUNTY LAWMEN, CIRCA 1880.

In *Manhunts & Massacres*, the second in the *Arizona Highways* Wild West Collection, history writers tell 18 exciting, true stories from Arizona's violent past. Some recount cleverly staged ambushes and horrible massacres. Others center on arduous expeditions across the Southwest's most hostile landscape to bring in elusive murderers. And in a few of these historical tales, the amazing part of the story is the legal machinations and delays that either kept killers from the noose for years or that incarcerated others long past the time required to pay for their crimes.

The map on Page 6 shows the locations where the stories in *Manhunts & Massacres* took place.

Twin Murders at Tuttle's Station

A pair of Army deserters committed twin murders so brutal that one of the killers had to change his blood-soaked shoes before fleeing. In the ensuing manhunt, an Old West sheriff abandoned the timeworn horseback posse and chased the murderers across northeastern Arizona in a Cadillac horseless carriage.

BY LEO W. BANKS

IT STARTED WITH AN ARGUMENT OVER A DOG, AND BEFORE THE matter was settled two men would be brutally murdered, lynch mobs would demand rope justice, and President Woodrow Wilson would order a dramatic, last-minute stay of execution. But in the end, killers William Stewart and John B. Goodwin would dangle at the bottom of government gallows in a case that still is debated in the lonesome outback of east-central Arizona's Gila County.

On September 14, 1910, a year and a half before Arizona became a state, deer hunters Fred Kibbe and Alfred Hillpot tied their horses outside Tuttle's Station, a stage stop and inn located along an old military supply road between Fort Apache and San Carlos in eastern Arizona.

Owner Bill Tuttle had turned operation of the station over to Stewart and Goodwin, unaware that both men were deserters from the U.S. Army. But Kibbe and Hillpot had no reason to suspect trouble. Stewart and Goodwin invited the hunters to lay over, offering to cook for them and care for their horses.

**SCENE OF THE MURDERS OF FRED KIBBE
AND ALFRED HILLPOT, CIRCA 1914.**

As they awaited the next day's hunting, Kibbe, 24, a grocer who'd married into a prominent Globe family, and Hillpot, about 27, a newcomer from New Jersey whose first name also was reported as Albert, chatted amiably with the two station managers.

But trouble began that same day when a dog belonging to Stewart bit Hillpot in the leg, and he responded by kicking the animal hard enough to draw a yelp. An argument erupted, but by the next day, the hunters assumed the incident was over, and set out to find deer, but were unsuccessful. On their way back to the station, they met three friends from Globe — Mr. and Mrs. M.E. Conboy and George Zimmerman — who'd camped for the night to cook the deer they'd shot.

Zimmerman and Conboy told Kibbe and Hillpot that they would come to Tuttle's Station the following morning and lead them to an area rich with deer. With that agreement made, Kibbe and Hillpot departed with steaks given them by Mrs. Conboy.

That night, Thursday, September 15, the two hunters

feasted on what would be their final meal — venison, beans, fried potatoes, hot biscuits, and jelly .

The gruesome story of what happened next came from Joseph E. Morrison, U.S. attorney for Arizona and a prosecutor in the subsequent case. His account was published 47 years later in the *Globe Arizona Record*.

It was right after supper, and Kibbe was sitting on a backless chair, leaning forward with his elbows on a table enjoying a smoke from his corncob pipe.

Goodwin, better known by the alias James Steele, rose from where he was sitting a few feet away, and with no provocation, drew a six-shooter and put a bullet into Kibbe's forehead, killing him instantly.

Then Stewart took up a .30-.30 Marlin rifle and began firing at Hillpot as he lay on his back on his bedroll with his head against a saddle. One shot penetrated Hillpot's torso, narrowly missing the heart. Another entered the middle of his left shoulder and exited at his armpit, and a third struck him in the neck.

But Hillpot was alive when the shooting stopped, so Stewart charged him and, using the rifle as a club, beat Hillpot so severely that the rifle's stock splintered and "portions of the brains and bone were dashed against the walls of the cabin," according to Morrison.

The killers hurried outside to steal their victims' horses, then decided to return to the cabin to rob the bodies of any valuables. Remarkably, Hillpot was not yet dead. To finish the job, Stewart drew a knife and cut his throat.

By that time, Stewart's shoes were so bloody that he yanked Hillpot's shoes off the still warm body and put them on. He and Goodwin mounted the horses and fled the station, carrying all of the hunters' belongings.

By the time Conboy and Zimmerman arrived at Tuttle's Station the morning after the killings, as promised, and notified the law of what they'd discovered, the killers had a 15-hour head start. The manhunt lasted seven days and might have

THE TOWN OF GLOBE, WHERE GOODWIN AND STEWART
WERE TRIED FOR MURDER BETWEEN 1910 AND 1914.
THIS STREET SCENE IS FROM LABOR DAY, 1911.

ended in failure if Kibbe and Hillpot hadn't chanced upon that second party of deer hunters the day before their deaths.

The killers were up against a formidable opponent in J.H. Thompson, known as the territory's senior sheriff and a cunning tracker of bad men. In previous cases, Thompson had earned a reputation for the peculiar contents of his saddlebags: an extra box of ammunition, a change of socks and underwear, and a box of salt. As the *Arizona Record* noted: "He [was] a great lover of this life sustaining substance."

This manhunt also marked the end of an era for Thompson. For the first time in his long career, he shunned his horse for an automobile. The sheriff contacted M.L. Naquin, owner of the first Cadillac automobile to appear on the streets of Globe, and convinced him to use that car as the chase vehicle. So Thompson — along with Naquin, "horseless carriage" mechanic S.T. "Red" Brewer, and District Attorney Walter Shute — drove off in high style to find the killers.

The Cadillac performed well on the pock-marked road but burned out a bearing just short of Tuttle's Station. This near disaster resulted in what press accounts described as heroic repair work by Brewer.

He went to an old sawmill and retrieved bearing metal from some abandoned machinery, melted the metal in a frying pan, and cast a bearing in sand. After many hours of work, Naquin's Caddy was up and running again.

The manhunt was several days along when Thompson's party found the getaway horses, exhausted and running loose about 20 miles east of Holbrook. The tip that led to the arrest came from an unlikely source, a barber in Holbrook named W.B. Cross.

He was cutting the hair of a Gila County cowboy, whose name has never been firmly established, when conversation turned to the ongoing manhunt. The cowboy mentioned that he'd just spotted two sets of tracks left by exhausted humans near the whistle-stop of Adamana, 25 miles east of Holbrook.

Hearing that, Cross dropped his scissors and bolted across the street to the telegraph office to alert Thompson. Capture came without incident on September 22, when Stewart and Goodwin went into a store in Adamana to buy supplies.

Thompson then loaded his prisoners onto a train for the trip back to Globe. En route, he learned that the mood in town had grown ugly and that a mob of 500 townsmen was meeting every incoming train. Fearing a necktie party, the shrewd sheriff transferred his prisoners to a car in Phoenix and spirited them safely back to Globe along the rugged Apache Trail flanking the Salt River.

Stewart and Goodwin were put on trial five separate times in a bizarre legal tangle that lasted four years. In the first two trials, both men were found guilty and sentenced to life in prison — Goodwin for killing Kibbe and Stewart for killing Hillpot. But defense lawyer Thomas E. Flannigan won a new trial by arguing that because the crimes were committed on an Indian reservation, with only white men involved, his clients had been convicted illegally by the trials in territorial court. The law required that the cases be heard in federal court.

Flannigan won his argument, but the results were disastrous. He ran up against U.S. Attorney Joseph Morrison, a fierce prosecutor who wanted both defendants to suffer the death penalty.

The best way to accomplish this, Morrison reasoned, was to re-indict the men for the most brutal of the two murders, which was Hillpot's. Success hinged on convincing the juries that both men were legally culpable for both murders.

Two more trials were held. Goodwin was convicted and given a death sentence, but Stewart, thanks to a single juror who couldn't abide capital punishment, was sentenced to life in a federal penitentiary in Atlanta.

Not content with letting Stewart live out his sentence, Morrison pulled an unprecedented legal maneuver and brought Stewart back from Atlanta to stand trial for killing Kibbe. This time Stewart, too, was sentenced to death.

This fifth and final trial produced an interesting side drama, a romance between prosecutor Morrison and Rose Kibbe, Fred's sister. Joe Morrison later married Rose Kibbe.

The killers' executions were recounted in the book, *Sheriff Thompson's Day*, by Jess G. Hayes, former Gila County superintendent of schools. Goodwin's hanging was originally scheduled for March 14, 1913, at the Gila County jail in Globe.

But Flannigan, racked with guilt at his legal gamble gone bad, scrambled to save his client's life by appealing directly to President Woodrow Wilson for executive clemency. Hours before the hanging was to occur, Wilson sent a telegram to Arizona, ordering a 60-day stay to study the issue.

With that delay, the fever of anticipation in Globe broke, and the tense deathwatch around the newly-built gallows ended. But before the crowd dispersed, souvenir seekers practically carried the gallows away in pieces.

But the execution was carried out as soon as the stay was over. Goodwin's last request to Flannigan was to be hanged wearing oxford shoes, new trousers, a white shirt with a black necktie, and a red rose on his breast.

"Pin it on my shirt so it won't fall off when I make the drop," Goodwin told his lawyer. "Bury me with it on."

Flannigan pinned on the rose, then Goodwin took the 13 steps to the gallows' platform two at a time. At the top he saw that his executioner was a local bill collector named Bill Cunningham, who was hired to spring the trapdoor, for a reported $50, by a fainthearted U.S. marshal and his deputy. Before dropping to his death, Goodwin cussed out the two absent federal lawmen for lacking the guts to do their job.

Stewart died in the same spot a year later, on May 29, 1914, also at the hand of hangman Cunningham. Stewart, too, was angry that the federal lawmen were absent. He confronted Cunningham on the gallows, saying, "I'll meet you in hell, and before you come to be with me, I hope you choke to death."

Writers have made frequent note that Cunningham, many years later, died from throat cancer.

The amateur executioner probably lived with Stewart's words rattling through his brain, and defense attorney Flannigan no doubt suffered the knowledge that if he would have let matters stand following the first trials, his clients would have remained alive, perhaps as free men after serving long terms.

Another odd aspect of this story was that Stewart was executed for killing Kibbe, and Goodwin for killing Hillpot, when the evidence was overwhelming that it happened the other way around.

But the strangest twist to these murders was the explanation of the killers that their terrible violence and blood lust stemmed from a dispute over a dog.

The Legend of Apache Leap

In the 1860s, when the Apache Indians were defending their homeland from the encroaching tide of white settlers, the U.S. Army surprised a large band of Apaches atop the high mountain east of the mining town of Superior. The short, pitched battle ended with the Apaches throwing themselves to their deaths from a thousand-foot-high cliff rather than surrender to the soldiers. While lack of documentation of the event has confounded historians for decades, storytellers throughout the West still repeat the tale.

BY JAMES E. COOK

━━◆◆◆━━

THE STORY OF APACHE LEAP ISN'T OFTEN TOLD NOW. IT isn't a pretty story; it goes back to the days when many white men looked upon Apaches as less than human. But the landmark and the name linger, wanting to be explained: Apache Leap.

Since the late 19th century, a vague story has persisted of 75 Apache warriors, trapped at the top of the cliff by pursuing soldiers, leaping to their deaths rather than surrendering.

There seems to be no official record of the story in military archives, and Apache historians have heard it only in the vague white men's versions. There may be some truth in the legend, but, as historian Dale Miles says, the lack of evidence is the kind of gap that drives writers and historians crazy.

Driving eastward from Apache Junction on U.S. Route 60 toward the mining town of Superior, you'll see the daunting, red-streaked bluff rising at the north end of the Dripping Springs Mountains. Apache Leap, a cliff made of sedimentary stone layers more than 230 million years old, towers 2,000 feet above Superior and the surrounding desert hills.

The U.S. Army established Camp Infantry, later called Camp Pinal, in the vicinity in 1870. In the spring of 1871, Col. George Stoneman, military commander of Arizona, ordered the outpost moved to the base of the vertical Picket Post Mountain six miles west of Superior and nearly as tall as 4,833-foot Apache Leap. The military named the new location Camp Picket Post. It protected and eventually merged with the mining camp called Pinal, or Pinal City, near the site of today's Boyce Thompson Southwest Arboretum State Park.

The Army, whose job it was to protect miners, freighters, and settlers from raids by Apaches, found the top of Picket Post to be an excellent site from which to observe movement in the area, and to send signals by heliograph (mirrors) to lookouts on other mountains.

Many of these newcomers to Arizona wouldn't have minded seeing the "hostiles" exterminated so settlers could build new lives in peace. The Apaches viewed it differently: They were using guerrilla warfare to defend their homeland from white aggressors.

The soldiers saw Apache campfires nightly on the top of the mountain then called Big Picacho — the one that would become known as Apache Leap. Big Picacho seemed a safe refuge from frontal attack. From it, the Indians kept a sharp eye on Camp Picket Post, but apparently not sharp enough.

Writer and photographer Dane Coolidge, well-known in his time, heard this version of the story told in 1903 at Pinal City:

"Pinal itself had been an army outpost, and from the towering summit of Picket Post, soldiers had watched the plains below, flashing the news to Tucson with their heliographs whenever they saw Indians on a raid.

"To get rid of these troops, the Tonto Apaches called all their warriors together, lighting hundreds of fires along the summit of a cliff that overlooked the post. But the bold captain did not wait for the Indians to attack.

"As soon as night fell he rode forth with all his men, and at dawn they jumped the Tonto camp. A few fought back but most of them leaped over the brink to their death on the rocks below, for which the cliff is called Apache Leap."

Writer C.S. Scott gave more detail in the October 1914 issue of the long-since-defunct *Arizona* magazine:

"The redskins and soldiers could plainly see each other from mountaintop to mountaintop, beyond the possible range of any arms that either had. The Indians felt secure, and the whites were merely carrying out a strategic plan."

Troops sneaked around the end of the mountains and came up on the east side of Big Picacho.

"By means of the heliograph they [soldiers at Picket Post] signaled to scouts of the mountain party, who were instructed to always keep the [Picket Post] party in view, apprising them of the whereabouts of the Indians.

"The mountain party then stealthily crept up on the farther side of the big mountain in the rear of the Apaches and assaulting them by surprise, wrought fearful havoc with their initial volley and followed up their bloody work as fast as possible."

In the article, Scott wrote that the Apache party included women and children.

"The Indians were panic-stricken and retreated in the only direction possible, toward the hither side of the mountain, which is a perpendicular cliff. It is said that many who did not fall before the rain of bullets threw themselves off the cliff in the hope of escaping fatal injury.

"Those of recent times who have been sufficiently curious and energetic to scale its forbidding cliff report the finding of beads, bones, and arrowheads, grim proofs of the essential facts of an incident of history that is fast entering the twilight zone between authentic detail and legendary recital."

Dale Miles, historian for the San Carlos Apache Tribe, said, "I've been hard put to find an Apache version of the story, either in oral or written histories." Of the white man's version, he said, "It seems implausible that something that momentous wouldn't have shown up in Army records. It has become a part of Southwest lore, but there's little verification to back it up."

He continued, "I'm inclined to think it's a made-up folktale. Maybe something like it happened, involving just two or three people, and the story snowballed."

Historian Dan L. Thrapp mentioned the legend in a footnote of his exhaustive book *Conquest of Apacheria*. Thrapp said he could find no report of the military action, but a local historian, now deceased, had assured him it was based in fact.

Thrapp brought it up because he was having trouble documenting a similar leap during the Battle of Turret Peak, in another part of Arizona. It was a pivotal action in Gen. George Crook's 1873 campaign against the Apaches.

Thrapp found no other report to support something Crook described in his autobiography: "Just at dawn of day our people fired a volley into their camp [atop the 5,400-foot mountain] and charged with a yell. So secure did [the Apaches] feel in this almost impregnable position that they lost all presence of mind, even running past their holes in the rocks. Some of them jumped off the precipice and were mashed into a shapeless mass."

So the story of Apache Leap is not beyond possibility. The legend has been used to promote the fable of "Apache tears," graceful perlite globules mined near Superior and used as jewelry.

One promotional document on file at the Arizona Mineral Museum in Phoenix links the Apache tears fable to a very specific military action in the winter of 1871. A Capt. John Walker is said to have led the Pima Indian troops of Company B, 1st Arizona Volunteers, on the raid atop Apache Leap.

"Nearly 50 of the band of 75 Apaches were killed in the

first volley of shots. The remainder of the tribe retreated to the cliff's edge and chose death by leaping over the edge rather than to die at the hands of the attackers."

The problem with that account is that the 1st Arizona Volunteers no longer existed in 1871. The militia unit, made up of Mexicans and Native Americans, was formed to track down "hostiles" in 1865, when most federal soldiers were away fighting in the Civil War. The volunteers never received a dime's pay and were disbanded early in 1866 after killing about 100 "hostiles."

During that same era, vigilante civilian armies, some pretty bloodthirsty, were afield to deal with "the Indian problem." If the incident at Apache Leap occurred in the 1860s, during the time of volunteers and vigilantes, then, Miles agreed: "It would be logical that fewer records were kept."

Another incident early in Thrapp's book supports that notion. Thrapp went back to the few records of the 1st Arizona Volunteers to tell of a Capt. John Walker leading the Pima Indians of Company C and 40 Maricopa Indians from Company B on a raid against Apaches. Twenty-five Apaches were killed. The attacking Volunteers, who also had been raided by Apaches, smashed in the faces of the dead Apaches.

That was early in 1866. Thrapp's skimpy sources said Walker's troops started from the Pima Villages, southwest of the Dripping Springs Mountains. Newspaper accounts said that some miners, whose presence was not explained, were disgusted by the bloodthirsty mutilations.

Could this have been the encounter that grew into the legend of Apache Leap? Whatever the root of the story, it seems lost in that zone "between authentic detail and legendary recital," offering only visions of stubborn warriors, but no detail of the time of their dramatic deaths.

CHAPTER THREE

It's Handy to Have a Sharp Knife

*At a remote outpost in Nevada, on the edge of
Death Valley, James Boone provoked immigrant
miner Antone Bacoch into a fight, stabbed him
22 times, and galloped into the night on a stolen
horse. Lawmen hired Indian trackers and
paroled claim jumper Jack Longstreet to hunt the
fugitive across southern Nevada and into
Arizona. But legendary Arizona Sheriff George
Ruffner got the drop on the killer near
Peach Springs, at the western end of the Grand
Canyon, and brought him in without a shot.*

BY SALLY ZANJANI

———◦—◦———

B Y LATE JANUARY 1896 IN YAVAPAI COUNTY, ARIZONA,
Sheriff George Ruffner had his suspicions. When the detailed description he had requested from Nevada law-enforcement officials arrived, those suspicions were confirmed. A teamster he had seen hauling ore from a copper mine on the Peach Springs road was really a killer with rewards totaling close to a thousand dollars on his head. The only remaining question for Ruffner was how to take the fugitive.

Two months earlier, the scattered settlers in Tule Canyon, Nevada, had been shocked by an unusually brutal murder. The victim was a Slav immigrant, Antone Bacoch; the killer was James Boone, a 41-year-old West Virginian and former railroad engineer who kept a few head of cattle and occasionally worked on the Slav's mining claims. At least, those were his nominal occupations. A good many denizens of the isolated communities on the fringes of the Death Valley region in those days were "on the dodge," and it was suggested by some that Boone was by no means out of place among the desperados.

The murder occurred late in the afternoon on Nov. 20, 1895. Boone had appeared in Bob Robinson's Tule Canyon store and remarked that he expected trouble with Bacoch. When one of the other customers asked him why he was sharpening his knife on his boot, Boone enigmatically replied, "It's handy to have a sharp knife."

By the time Bacoch arrived, it was nearly dark. Soon the two men began arguing over a trivial debt. When Boone made an ethnic slur against Slavs, Bacoch punched him and shoved him through the door into Robinson's living quarters behind the store. Robinson saw the two men struggling on the bunk. Boone was plunging his knife into Bacoch, while the Slav's hand still clutched his assailant's throat. Moments later, Bacoch tumbled to the floor, his head and body riddled with 22 stab wounds.

No one moved to stop the blood-spattered killer as he saddled Robinson's horse and galloped into the November darkness. Esmeralda County, Nevada, Sheriff William A. Ingalls, when informed of the killing, decided that he should remain in Hawthorne, where such urgent problems as liquor and opium sales to Indians demanded his immediate attention. Silver Peak Deputy Sam Wasson, more than 80 miles closer to the scene, took charge of the manhunt for Boone and called for Indian trackers, who lost little time in picking up Boone's trail. John Shakespeare, a Paiute tracker, later recalled: "Damn if I know how far I track him. . . . Sam Wasson tell me bring Boone back."

As Shakespeare's words implied, Deputy Wasson had quickly abandoned the search for Boone. He disbanded his posse of Indians and settlers, explaining that the fugitive had headed southeast into a region where pursuit was "almost impossible" due to stretches of terrain 40 to 60 miles long without feed or water. Otherwise, declared Wasson, he would, of course, have followed Boone all the way to the Colorado River.

It appears that Ingalls and Wasson felt less than enthusiastic about searching for Boone and perhaps actually finding him in some narrow defile, his clothes rusty with dried blood, sharpening his knife on his boot. Instead, they needed a man unfazed by danger, whether it came from the desert or from a showdown with a killer who could fight like a cornered mountain lion.

They summoned Jack Longstreet, the mysterious frontiersman with the well-notched Colt .44 who ranched in Ash Meadows, Nevada, on the eastern fringe of Death Valley. No one questioned the propriety of hiring as an agent of the law a man recently released from jail following his part in a claim jumping. And no one found it surprising that Longstreet hired on to hunt the murderer.

On the night of December 2, nearly two weeks after Boone took flight, an Indian courier appeared with letters from Longstreet suggesting that Boone might still be hiding somewhere in southern Nevada's Amargosa Valley, where witnesses had reported seeing a man with blackened eyes, skinned hands, and bloody clothes two days after the stabbing.

But Boone had not paused in his desperate flight. When he reached Stump Spring on the southwest rim of the Pahrump Valley, he somehow learned that Longstreet was on his trail.

This news kept him on the run, and his long lead enabled him to escape across the Colorado River into Arizona.

Believing that he had reached a safe haven where no one knew or cared about his identity, he began work as a freighter, driving teams between the Ridenour Mine and Peach Springs. But Boone had not reckoned on Sheriff Ruffner, who was hunting horse thieves in Mohave County. Unspecified "peculiar actions" by the new teamster reminded the sheriff of a reward notice that had recently crossed his desk concerning a big man, "rawboned" and "straight built," with a sandy mustache and pale-blue eyes.

Once certain, Sheriff Ruffner concluded that the best way to arrest the fugitive without arousing his suspicions was to take him on alone without the assistance of a posse, or even his deputies. Pretending to be a butcher in search of mutton, Ruffner hitched his team behind the lead wagon in a caravan of three on the Peach Springs road and swung up to ride with the driver. Boone's wagon brought up the rear.

After they had jolted along together for several miles, Ruffner told the teamster beside him who he was. The man warned that Boone kept a Winchester in his wagon. Undeterred, Ruffner ordered the teamster to stop and grease his wagon, which brought Boone's wagon creaking to a halt behind them. The unsuspecting Boone dismounted and sauntered up to the "butcher," who instantly whipped out a six-shooter, thrust it against Boone's chest, and commanded him to surrender. Only when the manacles were locked in place and the sheriff had found proof of his identity did Boone's protests finally collapse.

After the circuitous train trip by which Ruffner delivered his prisoner to Nevada, Boone's defense attorney served him better than had his Winchester or his knife.

The murder trial in late April 1896 resulted in a verdict of not guilty, despite considerable evidence of premeditation. Whether Sheriff Ruffner regarded this result as coddling criminals is not known. He was undoubtedly well-aware that the usual outcome of a frontier homicide trial was an acquittal on grounds of self-defense and went on doing his job all the same.

Boone, for his part, could count himself lucky, not only in his acquittal, but also in the manner of his arrest. The last time Longstreet went after a fugitive, the suspected horse thief later was found dead by the side of the road. If Boone had to be captured, he stood a better chance of survival at the hands of Sheriff Ruffner.

Antonio Narbona and Massacre Cave

*Navajo raiders attacked the Spanish colony
of Seboyeta twice in 1804, killing settlers
and stealing sheep. The Spanish retaliated,
sending nearly 300 men under Lt. Antonio
Narbona to Canyon de Chelly to punish the
Navajos. The story of the resulting massacre,
complete with warnings from talking
coyotes, is still told on long nights on the
Navajo reservation of northern
Arizona and New Mexico.*

BY   SUSAN   HAZEN-HAMMOND

I N JANUARY 1800, IN THE DAYS WHEN SPAIN CLAIMED THE
Southwest, and her colonial villages sat like islands in an
Indian sea, New Mexico Governor Fernando Chacón gave
130 families from Albuquerque permission to move roughly
40 miles westward. They settled an area called Seboyeta, east
of the Navajos' sacred Mt. Taylor and north of the Indian homes
at Laguna Pueblo. Around a central plaza, they built a fortress-
like village of stone and hardened mud. They planted corn and
herded sheep and cattle. They traded, worshipped, and so-
cialized with their Indian neighbors.

One night in April 1804, a party of 200 Navajos broke
through the fortified walls of Seboyeta. They ransacked three
homes, killed three shepherds, took a boy prisoner, and stole
more than a hundred horses, cows, and sheep.

For weeks Navajo raiders harassed Spanish and Pueblo Indian villagers across New Mexico. By May 16, they had stolen more than 3,000 pregnant ewes and killed nine shepherds. In June, Comandante Gen. Nemesio Salcedo in Chihuahua ordered Governor Chacón to pursue the Navajos and not make peace "until we are able to chastise them."

On August 3, a group of 900 to 1,000 Navajos attacked Seboyeta again. This time, the colonists abandoned their homes and crops and fled south to Laguna Pueblo. Salcedo ordered them to return home or lose their lands. Then he began moving troops from the south to fight the Navajos.

Still, the raids continued.

Finally, in October, Salcedo ordered a lieutenant named Antonio Narbona to leave his post at Tubac, south of Tucson, and join the campaign against the Navajos. Narbona, 31, had been born in Mobile, Alabama, when it was still Spanish territory. By the time he was 13, he had begun his career as a soldier in what is today southern Arizona. In the spring of 1795, at age 21, he traveled as second in command of an exploring party that pushed north through Apache country from Tucson to Zuni Pueblo in search of a better trade route between Tucson and Santa Fe.

Obeying his orders in October 1804, the young officer recruited soldiers from Tucson, Santa Cruz, Tubac, and other Sonoran outposts, then led them north. On November 26, Narbona wrote from near Laguna Pueblo that he was about to set out for Navajo country with 180 Sonoran troops and 102 New Mexican auxiliaries, including two Zuni guides.

On December 3, at the foot of the hills at the upper end of Canyon de Chelly, in eastern Arizona, Narbona's troops attacked a small Navajo settlement, killing one man and taking a man, a woman, and a girl as prisoners.

In his report to Chacón on the battle, Narbona wrote that he was full of "embarrassment and shame" that he hadn't done better, but the snow was so bad that "neither the cavalry nor the infantry could continue"; horses were exhausted, and the soldiers' feet were swollen. Narbona implied that he would certainly understand if Chacón sent him home to Sonora.

Instead, the governor ordered him back to the field. Narbona arranged for fresh provisions, including cigars for the soldiers, and planned his next attack.

This time Narbona and his men rode down into Canyon de Chelly. Early on January 17, they encountered Navajos, and a battle began.

The Navajos had entrenched themselves in what Narbona called "an almost inaccessible, fortified place." The two sides fought all that day and again the following morning, and the Spanish shot off almost all their ammunition — more than 10,000 rounds.

By fighting with what Narbona described as "the greatest ardor and diligence," he and his men won the battle, "killing 90 warriors and 25 women and children." Prisoners included an important Navajo leader, Segundo, and his wife and two children. Spanish casualties were limited to one dead and 64 wounded.

In his report to Chacón, Narbona commended the New Mexicans who fought with him. "Cpl. Baltasar Ribera brings 84 pairs of ears of as many warriors," he added, and apologized that six pairs had been lost. Then Narbona and his Sonoran soldiers headed south.

Meanwhile, back at Canyon de Chelly, Navajos mourned their friends, brothers, sisters, mothers, fathers, lovers, and children. And they repeated again and again the story of the battle. Over the decades, as the ink of Narbona's reports and letters faded, the northernmost Spanish colonies in the Americas became part of the new country of Mexico, then the United States. Navajos suffered atrocities and abuses that made earlier conflicts seem mild. But year after year, generation after generation, tribal storytellers retold the tale of the encounter with Narbona. The place where the battle was said to have occurred acquired the name *Adah Aho'doo'nilí*, the "place where two fell off." In English, it became known as Massacre Cave.

THE NAVAJOS AT CANYON DE CHELLY, WHERE THIS
NAVAJO FAMILY WAS PHOTOGRAPHED IN THE LATE 1800S,
WERE NOT PART OF A CENTRALIZED NAVAJO NATION.

Veronica Tsosie Yoe, a sturdy Navajo medicine woman in
her late 20s, works as a guide at Canyon de Chelly. As a child,
sometimes she would sit up all night listening to her grand-
mother tell stories in Navajo. One of those stories is about
Massacre Cave.

"The warriors were off hunting. Only the elderlies and
the women and kids were left behind. They were hiding in a
cave right across from Coyote Point, and the Spanish people
couldn't see them. Every morning early, an old lady who had
been captured by the Spanish people when she was a little girl
would go out on the ledge and talk to a coyote across the way.
He was giving the people a message that the Spanish people
were going to come. But when this lady saw the Spanish people

in the bottom of the canyon, she started yelling them out. That's
how the Spanish people knew the people were there. If that
lady wouldn't have started screaming, it wouldn't have happened. I guess it was meant to happen."

Harry Walters, an anthropologist and the director of
Hatathli Museum at Navajo Community College, analyzes both
sides of the massacre.

"I have a problem with the Spanish documents. I think
they altered the figures. They say 900 warriors raided Seboyeta,
but historically we Navajos have never raided in such large
parties. And they say they killed almost four times as many
warriors as women and children. But there were never more
warriors than women and children and elderly.

"I heard this a few years ago from an elder who lived in
the area. He said the day before the incident, a man was hunting rabbits on top of the ridge. He was walking along the trail
when he heard someone up ahead saying to himself, 'It looks
very bad. There's going to be a great catastrophe soon.' So the
hunter hid in the bushes to see who that man was."

When the speaker arrived, it was a coyote.

"The fact the coyote was talking was out of the ordinary.
The message was serious. If the hunter had related it to the
people, they could have done the Protection Way ceremony,
and everything would have been different. They would have
said, this is a bad place to hide. Let's find it somewhere else.
That's what it means when a coyote crosses your path. It means
wait a minute. It means maybe what you are planning is not the
correct way to do something. Maybe you should get a second
opinion. But the hunter didn't tell anyone about meeting the
coyote. It was two days after the battle before the man came
back and discovered the corpses.

"The Navajo perspective is of a massacre of innocent people who had nothing to do with the raid."

Historians on all sides of the issue agree that the raiders,
whoever they were, probably didn't come from Canyon de Chelly.
So why did Narbona head for the canyon both times? Probably

because the Spanish considered the Navajos from a European perspective, as a centralized nation, rather than as a series of loosely affiliated bands. Writers of the era called Canyon de Chelly the Navajo capital. To the Spanish, it made sense to strike the capital.

Today there's no certainty whether the written accounts of colonial officials are more or less reliable than the oral accounts of the Navajos. Or why the Navajos attacked Seboyeta and other villages. Or whether, as Navajo tradition holds, the man who led the Navajo raids against Seboyeta and other villages in the spring and summer of 1804 was a famous Navajo leader who himself went by the name Narbona. (Historians also do not agree on how the Navajo Narbona acquired his name or what connection, if any, existed between him and Antonio Narbona.)

We do know that after the incident at Canyon de Chelly, the Navajos and the Spanish colonists negotiated a peace that lasted, with lapses, until 1817.

Meanwhile, Antonio Narbona went on to become one of the most prominent frontiersmen of his time, serving as governor of Sonora and later, of New Mexico. As far as we know, he never wrote down his personal feelings about what happened at Canyon de Chelly; the nearest we can come to knowing them are the words inscribed in a sundial he ordered erected on the plaza in Santa Fe when he was governor: *Vita fugit sicut umbra*, "Life flees like a shadow."

CHAPTER FIVE

Augustine Chacón, *Hombre Muy Bravo*

*Robber, horse thief, and self-proclaimed killer
of 14 men, Augustine Chacón broke out of his
cell and eluded the law for five years.
On the day he finally faced the noose,
he did so with cool indifference. He ate a hearty
breakfast and lunch and strolled to the gallows.
Once atop the platform, he asked for a cup of coffee
and a cigarette and casually addressed
the crowd below for more than half an hour
before it was his time to hang.*

BY SAM NEGRI

I N AN OLD CEMETERY IN THE TINY COMMUNITY OF SAN JOSÉ, Arizona, near the Gila River, Augustine Chacón lies buried under a marble gravestone. Because of the tidy marker, the location of Chacón's grave in the middle of the cemetery, roughly 10 feet from a flagpole, and Chacón's relatively young age — he was 41 or 42 when he died — it's easy to get the impression that he was some kind of hero. But historian Jay J. Wagoner described Chacón as "a bloodthirsty, ruthless killer unparalleled in Arizona's criminal annals."

Many regard the crime for which Chacón finally was executed as the most sensational episode in the history of Morenci, a rough-and-tumble eastern Arizona copper mining town. Typical of many incidents during Arizona's territorial days, accounts of precisely what occurred there on the night of December 18, 1895, vary in their details, though the broader elements are consistent.

Paul Robert Becker, a German immigrant, was managing Mrs. McCormick's General Store in Morenci. Shortly before midnight three men, later identified as Chacón, Pilar Luna, and Dinnicido Morales, entered the store through a rear window.

Becker said Chacón hit him on the head with a gun and ordered him to open a safe. Most accounts say Becker resisted and tried to yank the gun away from one or more of his attackers, but Al Fernandez, who was born in 1902, said he heard a different version from the sheriff's deputy who arrested Chacón the next day.

"When I was a kid, I took care of Alex Davis during the last five years of his life," Fernandez said. "Alex was the deputy in that area where Mrs. McCormick's store was. He told me that Chacón had a knife and he told Paul Becker to go over and open the safe. Well, Paul got so scared he forgot the combination, and Chacón thought he was stalling, so he stabbed him in the back."

While Chacón and his accomplices fled, Becker, with a 6-inch blade stuck in his side, stumbled out of the store and got as far as Salcido's Saloon, where Alex Davis removed the knife. Becker, who survived, had been stabbed twice and slashed five times.

Davis couldn't pursue Chacón in darkness, but the following morning he picked up a trail of bloodstains that started at Mrs. McCormick's store and continued up a steep hill nearby. The blood splotches led the lawman directly to the home of Santiago Contreras.

William Ryder Ridgeway, a Graham County historian, wrote:

"As he [Davis] approached the house . . . Chacón, Morales, and Luna were seen to flee, pursuing a southwesterly direction up a hill. Davis later testified he was fired upon by Pilar Luna at this time, initiating what proved to be Morenci's most memorable gun battle. The officer returned the fire and was joined quickly in the fray by Morenci's Justice of the Peace, Albert Brewer, who was about 100 yards to the rear at the time Chacón and his henchmen fled the Contreras home."

Davis popped off six rounds, evidently without hitting anyone, and paused to reload. When he started shooting again, he managed to wound but not stop Chacón. Chacón and his companions then climbed behind some rocks, forcing Davis to pursue a different course. As he started back down the hill, he ran into Pablo Salcido, a Morenci merchant who wanted to continue pursuing the trio up the hill.

Davis reportedly said, "No, let's get some guns and go around the hill. One of them is either killed or wounded."

Davis did just that, but Salcido continued up the hill and was killed by a single bullet in the forehead.

Witnesses said about 300 shots were exchanged in the battle. When the smoke cleared and Chacón was captured, he was suffering from a severe wound to his left arm and a lesser one to his chest. His two companions were dead.

Authorities charged Chacón with the murder of Pablo Salcido, who had once been his friend, and removed him from Morenci to the Graham County Jail, five miles east of Safford at Solomonville (the town's name has since been shortened to Solomon).

The case went to trial before presiding Judge Owen T. Rouse on May 26, 1896, and concluded May 28. Chacón's three court-appointed attorneys tried to prove their client had been severely wounded by the time Salcido was killed and that Pilar Luna had fired the fatal shot. Luna, of course, was dead and offered no defense.

The court did not buy Chacón's story. He was found guilty and sentenced to hang on July 24. Chacón's lawyers immediately filed an appeal with the Territorial Supreme Court. While awaiting the court's ruling, Graham County officers transferred Chacón to the Tucson jail, 135 miles to the west, because they suspected some of his friends would try to set him free. After the high court affirmed the conviction, Chacón was returned to

AUGUSTINE CHACÓN WHILE IN PRISON.

the Solomonville jail. Evidently, he had not been idle during the ride back. At Bowie Station, roughly 50 miles south of Solomonville, officers discovered Chacón's shackles had been sawed nearly in half.

Nearly a year after his original sentencing and appeal, Chacón again stood before Judge Rouse, who resentenced him to hang, this time on June 18, 1897. But Chacón was not ready to die. Nine days before his date with the rope, he waited until dark and dug his way through the jail's adobe walls, entered the vacant sheriff's office, pushed open a window, and vanished.

It took a little more than five years before the law caught up with Chacón, and one newspaper reported he had killed another four people in the interim. Chacón's recapture remains one of the stranger law-enforcement stories of territorial days.

The principal actors in this event were Capt. Burt

Mossman, of the Arizona Rangers, and Burt Alvord and Billy Stiles, two peace officers who had led a Jekyll-and-Hyde existence, enforcing the law while simultaneously arranging train robberies. Alvord, who was friends with Chacón, had escaped from the Tombstone jail in 1900. He would be particularly useful to Mossman because he knew the location of Chacón's hideout. Stiles had avoided trial by testifying against his accomplices.

Mossman conspired with Stiles to contact Alvord, who would lure Chacón to a trap on the Mexican side of the border. Using Stiles as a go-between, Mossman, posing as an escaped prisoner, got a message to Chacón that he wanted his help in stealing horses from Col. William C. Greene's ranch at Hereford, a stone's throw north of the border.

On the run for years from the hangman's noose, Chacón was understandably wary, but he eventually agreed to meet Alvord's "friend." Mossman rode across the border into Mexico for his covert encounter with the fugitive.

During their meeting, Chacón was described as restless and suspicious, especially when Alvord, who didn't want to be around when the arrest was made, suddenly disappeared. According to a prearranged plan, Mossman asked Chacón for a cigarette, then lit it with a stick from the campfire. Mossman threw down the stick as if he had been burned and rubbed his hand on his leg. From there it was a short move to his pistol, and Mossman had the drop on Chacón.

Although his commission as an Arizona Ranger had expired four days earlier and, in any case, he clearly had no authority south of the border, Mossman arrested Chacón and brought him across the border on horseback, handcuffed and with a rawhide rope around his neck. The lawman flagged down a train and took his prisoner to Benson, where he turned him over to Graham County Sheriff Jim Parks. Mossman then went to New York for a vacation to avoid being around while the Chacón case was being finalized.

Back in Solomonville, Chacón found that his old cell had

JUDGE OWEN T. ROUSE SENTENCED CHACÓN TO HANG.

been remodeled. This time, he was placed in a steel cage, shackled, and watched constantly. Despite attempts by his friends to get his sentence commuted to life imprisonment, Chacón was again ordered to be executed by hanging. Sheriff Parks had the gallows built by John Besner, a Solomonville blacksmith.

Chacón began November 21, 1902, his last day on earth, with a big breakfast. Then he met with Sixto Molino and Jesus Bustos, two of his close friends from nearby Buena Vista (a community about a mile north of present-day San Jose), and asked them to take care of his burial. Next he had a long conversation with a Catholic priest.

At noon, he ordered and received a large lunch. Then at 2 P.M., freshly shaved and dressed in a new black suit, Chacón left his cell and walked behind a sheriff and two deputies to the gallows erected in a courtyard. An estimated 50 people stood below, and many more had climbed into the nearby trees to watch the hanging of a man who once bragged of having killed 42 people in the course of his brief life.

Standing on the scaffold with the noose dangling behind him, Chacón asked for a cup of coffee, rolled a cigarette, and launched into a speech.

"I have much to say," he declared, and spent the next 10 minutes denying he had committed many of the crimes of which he'd been accused.

"I have a clear conscience," he told the spectators. Raising his right arm, he added, "I am sure that this hand has never been guilty of murder. I may have stolen and done a good many other things, but I am innocent of this crime."

Albert Sames, a lawyer who recorded Chacón's last words, noted that he spoke for a total of about 30 minutes, asked for another cigarette, and then sat down on the scaffold declaring, "It is nothing but right that when one is going to die that he be given a few moments of time to quietly smoke a cigarette." He glanced disdainfully at the crude coffin near the gallows.

"Is that all?" an interpreter asked him.

"*Sí, es todo,*" he replied. Yes, that's all.

Friends then came up to shake his hand and say good-bye. At one point Chacón turned to the sheriff and asked that he be allowed to live until 3 P.M., but was told his time was up.

"It's too late now," he told those still waiting to shake his hand. "Time to hang."

He removed his shoes, asked the sheriff if he was ready, and dropped through the trap to his death. Two doctors from Safford pronounced him dead within 16 minutes of the hanging.

For many years after Chacón's death, it was rumored that Sixto Molino and Jesus Bustos, who claimed the body, put Chacón in a wagon and sped away to San Jose, where vigorous but futile attempts were made to revive the corpse with whiskey and massages.

While the passage of nearly a century has dimmed the memory of Chacón's bloody crimes, his fearless demeanor on the day he was executed still is remembered in the borderlands.

A report in Solomonville's *Arizona Bulletin* in 1902 sums up the reason: "A nervier man than Augustine Chacón never walked to the gallows, and his hanging was a melodramatic spectacle that will never be forgotten by those who witnessed it."

Or for that matter, those who heard about it in family legend generations later. In April 1980, a group of Chacón's relatives from his birthplace in Sonora, as well as at least one from Phoenix, gathered at San José to dedicate a marble marker at his grave site. It reads:

> AUGUSTINE CHACÓN
> 1861-1902
> He lived life without fear
> He faced death without fear
> HOMBRE MUY BRAVO

But, while the killer and thief Augustine Chacón lived and died without fear, the same could not be said for his innocent victims.

CHAPTER SIX

The Goddard Station Murders

Two Mexican men entered Charles Goddard's
stage station just as he and his family
were sitting down to dinner. They
opened fire, mortally wounding
Charles Goddard and killing an employee,
then terrorized the survivors from outside
the station for three hours before fleeing
into the night. The ensuing manhunt covered
most of southern Arizona, but the fugitives
made it to Mexico and eluded justice for months
until lawmen finally tricked the murderers
into crossing the border.

BY LEO W. BANKS

⟩⟩⟨⟨

C HARLES GODDARD, PROPRIETOR OF GODDARD'S STATION, A stage stop and store about 50 miles north of Phoenix on the Black Canyon Road, sat down to supper at about 7 P.M. on a quiet Sunday. The front door opened without a knock and two Mexican men entered. One of them was tall, smooth-shaved, with a scar on his cheek. The other had a mustache. Both were heavyset and wore blue overalls and duck coats. If they looked like trouble, Goddard didn't spot it.

"*Que quiera?*" (What do you want) asked Goddard, standing up.

"*Cena*," (Supper) said the tall, scar-faced one.

THIS 1880S STAGE TO GILLETTE WAS ONE OF THOSE TRAVERSING THE BLACK CANYON ROAD, WHICH RAN PAST GODDARD'S STATION.

"*Dispense me*," (Excuse me) said Goddard and told the two Mexicans to wait until the family had finished its supper. Then Mrs. Goddard would get them something to eat.

"*Bueno*," (Good) said the tall one, who then buried his hand in his pocket.

Milton Turnbull, an invalid miner and one of the other parties in the room — which included Goddard's wife, his brother, Frank, and station teamster Frank Cox — would later say he thought the tall Mexican was reaching for money to pay for his food.

But what appeared in his hand was a six-shooter. His accomplice drew a gun, too. Then came the flashes of shots being fired, darkness from the lamp crashing to the floor, frantic people diving for cover, desperate shouting, death.

Two days would pass before Arizonans received a full accounting of the shooting at Goddard's Station on February 1, 1903. When they did, they reacted with understandable shock, and newspapers printed the truth when they called the deed cold butchery.

The delay was caused by what happened after the Mexicans emptied their weapons and left the station. For reasons investigators could never unravel, they didn't depart the area for at least three hours.

Their victims, those left breathing, spent a night of unimaginable fear, first watching the killers from the station window, then, after a few hours when they were no longer visible, watching the darkness, not sure if the assassins were still about.

Turnbull sat by a window with a shotgun in his lap. If the two attackers returned to finish the job, he intended to get off the first shots.

At one point, Mrs. Goddard went to a second-floor window and shouted, "Bloody murder!" in the direction of a miner's camp about 400 yards away.

The only reply she received came from one of the two shooters who shouted back something unintelligible in Spanish.

Turnbull, who said he could see the men reloading their weapons by the light of Goddard's store a short distance away, convinced Mrs. Goddard to step away from the window, lest they shoot her, too.

But she could be forgiven a bout of irrationality, because on the couch in the station parlor lay her husband, racked with pain, a bullet hole just below his heart.

What transpired in that station room after the shooting started was unknowable, even to the survivors. Everyone was left in total darkness when the table lamp overturned in the first spasms of chaos.

Turnbull and Mrs. Goddard refrained from relighting the lamp out of fear that it would make them better targets to the men outside.

Not until dawn did they realize that they'd spent a dark night with a dead man, Frank Cox. He was found sitting in his chair with his head dropped onto the table, a knife and fork still in his hands. Cox had been shot once in the right temple and again in the back of the neck.

"The assassin stood so close in firing the shots that the right side of the man's face is filled with powder and his shirt was powder burned," reported *The Arizona Republican*.

Turnbull told police he thought Cox had gotten away to

summon help. He also told investigators that at least five shots were fired and that he survived by diving under the table and playing dead.

The killers shot at but missed Mrs. Goddard as she ran and another bullet struck the back of Frank Goddard's chair just as he dove out of it.

He scrambled into an adjoining room where weapons were kept. But the darkness made it fruitless for him to return to confront the gunmen.

Mrs. Goddard spent the early part of the night listening to her husband's pleas for hot cloths, which she was unable to bring him. Near midnight, Charles Goddard declared that his end was coming, and in a tortured voice told his wife to remember that it was the tall, scar-faced man who shot him. He died Monday morning.

Mrs. Goddard's plight outraged Sheriff W.W. Cook of Maricopa County, who told *The Republican*: "The agony of those people being cooped up all night without any chance to do anything for the dying was something awful."

Cook joined with Sheriff Joseph Roberts of Yavapai County in mounting a manhunt. Early investigation turned up evidence that two men presumed to be the killers had purchased Colt revolvers at a secondhand store in Prescott the Friday night before the murders. Men answering the description also stopped at Cordes Station on Sunday and had a meal before continuing south to Goddard's place, arriving about noon.

Much of their time before the early-evening shooting was spent in the company of a Mexican who had come to the station hoping to find work at the sheep-shearing camp that Goddard ran there. A few minutes before the shooting, he was seen sitting on a bench outside the station, and when the killings were done, he fled. He was not believed involved in the murders, but all points were alerted to bring him in for questioning.

Within three days, with headlines blaring Governor Alexander Brodie's offer of a $500 reward, lawmen learned that the killers had been spotted in Phoenix, near Five Points. They

**FRANCISCO RENTERIA WAS PHOTOGRAPHED
WHILE JAILED IN PRESCOTT.**

promised imminent capture. But they were wrong, and the time that elapsed allowed several unfounded rumors time to flower.

One held that Goddard had experienced some trouble with the men before the shooting, and they'd returned to exact revenge. But on his deathbed, Goddard told his wife that he'd never seen them before. Another rumor told of Goddard's involvement in a fight at the station, in which a man identified only as Montez tried to kill another man with a set of shears. In disarming Montez, Goddard hit him over the head with a rifle, and Montez departed the scene making loud threats to return and kill the station owner. Initial investigation centered on Montez, but police eventually found that he was far away at another sheep camp at the time of the killings.

Motive troubled the police from the start. Speculation centered on robbery, but nothing was taken, even though opportunity was ample, and the question "why?" remains to this day unanswered.

That left lawmen with one thin thread to follow — look

**HILARIO HIDALGO'S PROMINENT SCAR
MARKED HIM AS GODDARD'S KILLER.**

for a tall, scar-faced Mexican. Over several weeks, investigators focusing on that single characteristic managed to pull in a number of men whose faces bore even the remotest marks. And each time, Mrs. Goddard was summoned to a dreary jail room to relive the worst night of her life and decide if this was the man.

The break came early in May with a tip that the men had been found working as railroad section hands in Naco, Sonora. Unable to make the arrests in Mexico, lawmen devised a ruse to lure them into Arizona. The (Prescott) *Arizona Journal-Miner* reported that one of the men was arrested when his work crew was given a job on the U.S. side of the line, although that was unknown to the killer.

"He supposed he was still in Mexican territory," wrote the *Journal-Miner*.

As for the second man, it was arranged for him to receive his pay in a check that could only be cashed at a Douglas, Arizona, bank. This suspect, too, was taken into custody as soon as he crossed the international line.

The long-sought-after killers were identified as Hilario Hidalgo and Francisco Renteria. They had worked on the grade of the Crown King Railroad and had been discharged the day before the killings.

The men admitted to nothing and pled not guilty. Only a few witnesses were called by the prosecution, but their testimony, especially that of Mrs. Goddard, was absolute and irrefutable.

"The scene was a most pathetic one when she pointed out the ruthless murderers of her husband," wrote the *Journal-Miner*.

Frank Goddard and Milton Turnbull also made positive identifications, as did Francisco Hernandez, the man who was with the killers most of the afternoon of February 1 and saw them go into the house a few minutes before the shots were fired.

The trial, as *The Republican* cryptically noted, "was a model of brevity." Within a month of the capture, the jury spoke, and the executions were set for July 31 in the yard of Yavapai County Jail.

At 10:45 that morning, Sheriff Roberts, an interpreter, and a newspaper reporter entered the jail to read the death warrant to the prisoners. A crowd, described by the *Journal-Miner* as "morbid," had already gathered around the gallows, and an estimated 500 more dangled from surrounding rooftops.

But the dark atmosphere had no effect on Roberts, who read the document "without any emotion or tremor to his voice."

When Hidalgo heard his fate, he laughed and remarked, "If that was a song, I could sing it to you now." He was evidently referring to the quantities of legal mumbo jumbo he'd heard throughout his trial, which was so great he'd committed it to memory.

The men proceeded to the gallows looking crisp and good, perhaps better than they ever had. They were clean, well-shaved, and wore new suits.

"Neither looked a hardened criminal as might be supposed from the merciless crime committed by them," wrote the *Journal-Miner*.

**RENTERIA AND HIDALGO AT THE GALLOWS
IN THE LAST MINUTES BEFORE THEIR HANGING.**

The paper added that their attitude toward eternity had undergone a change, too:

"While they had been utterly indifferent to all spiritual ministrations until the last few days, they both seemed to take deep interest today in the holy ministrations of the father."

The priest, Father Quetu, accompanied the condemned men to the scaffold, where they fell to their knees to accept his last measure of goodness. They exhibited what the papers called "rare nerve" as their hands and legs were bound. As the black hoods were being yanked over their heads and the supreme moment approached, the two called, *"Adios todos!"* to acquaintances in the throng.

The *Journal-Miner* wrote that when Roberts jerked the lever, Hidalgo and Renteria "shot downward with great velocity." *Adios*, indeed.

CHAPTER SEVEN

Ambush
in Guadalupe Canyon

*At daybreak at least 25 men, identified as
Mexican soldiers, ambushed seven cowboys
in southeastern Arizona's Guadalupe Canyon.
Five cowboys were killed either in their sleep
or as they scrambled to escape the bloodbath.
But what prompted the Guadalupe Canyon
Massacre? Was it revenge for a stagecoach holdup
and double murder? Or for the
murder and robbery of Mexican smugglers,
or for the torture and murder of
Mexican cowboys? And was it really the
Mexican Army that committed the heinous crime?
These questions have been the source of
curiosity and conjecture in southern Arizona
for more than a century.*

BY LEO W. BANKS

D AWN HAD JUST BROKEN ON AUGUST 13, 1881, WHEN THE
guns began to roar. At least 25 gunmen lined the rocky
rim of southeastern Arizona's Guadalupe Canyon, firing
down on their prey.

Below were seven cowboys, some still sleeping in their
tarp-covered bedrolls. Bullets popped into the ground around
them like raindrops. But some hit their mark, and five of the

cowboys met quick deaths. Imagine the terror the five must have known — waking up and seeing the flash of rifles, realizing that this was the day they would die.

For more than a century, this brief and brutal event has left historians and the curious shaking their heads in wonder, knowing that the essential question about what came to be called the Guadalupe Canyon Massacre could never be answered definitively.

Why did it happen? What motivated the murder of five cowboys engaged in the seemingly innocent work of driving a herd of cattle to market in Tombstone?

The drive began the morning of August 12 from the Animas Valley of southwestern New Mexico. Ranchers Billy Lang and Dixie Lee Gray decided that the border area was getting too hot and they had to get out. Shoot-outs among Mexican and American smuggling gangs were becoming more frequent, and word had spread that hostile Apaches were about to ride the warpath.

Figuring to play it safe, Gray and Lang gathered their herds and started west for Tombstone. They planned to sell the cattle and use the money to hole up until it was safe to return to their ranches.

Accompanying them were cowboys Billy Byers, Harry Ernshaw, and Charles Snow. Newman Haynes Clanton, patriarch of the notorious Clanton family, also was along on the trip.

In the early 1870s, newspapers often described "Old Man" Clanton as an upstanding southern Arizona farmer. Even so, strong rumors persisted that he headed a cutthroat, cross-border rustling gang that included his son, Ike, who fought the Earps at the O.K. Corral.

But in August 1881, Newman Clanton also performed the legitimate work of freighting supplies by wagon from Tombstone to Animas Valley ranchers.

The seventh man on the cattle drive was James "Slim Jim" Crane, a desperado and sometime cowboy alleged to have taken part in a March 15, 1881, stagecoach holdup near Benson in which two men were killed.

Crane, who worked for Clanton and was an enemy of the Earps, joined the drive along the way, explaining that he was headed for Mexico and wanted a place to camp for the night.

It would be his final sleep. Crane probably died without getting out of his bedroll. So fast and silent was the assault that the same can be said for Gray. Clanton was dressing beside his chuck wagon when the shooting started, and he most likely fell in the early hail of bullets.

A graphic account of the slaughter came from Billy Byers, who said Charley Snow was the first to die. Something had spooked the cattle and, thinking it might be a bear, Lang ordered Snow to ride up a small hill and have a look. The first shot of the fight sent him hurtling from his saddle, dead.

What happened next, according to survivor Byers, was given a full airing in the *Tombstone Nugget* newspaper:

"When they first fired and killed Snow I thought the boys were firing at a bear, jumped out of my blankets, and as I got up the boys around me were shot.

"As soon as I saw what was up I looked for my rifle, and not seeing it I grabbed my pistol, and seeing them shooting at us from all sides, started to run, but I didn't fall, and in a few more steps was hit in the arm, knocking the pistol out of my hand and I fell down."

At this time, Lang and Ernshaw tried to escape into the canyon and were met with a full volley from the attackers. Lang collapsed as he ran, his legs dotted with bullet holes. Still, he managed to empty his pistol at the assailants, killing one and wounding another before meeting his own end.

Ernshaw somehow did escape, in spite of a bullet in his abdomen. Byers, who reported that Lang was the only cowboy to do much fighting, continued: "You must remember that the reason we had no chance to fight was that the Mexicans had crawled up behind the low hills, and being almost over us fired right down among us.

"We could see nothing but little whiffs of smoke. I saw some Mexicans coming from the direction Will and Harry had run, wearing their hats and I thought they had been killed or lost their hats in getting away."

But for Byers, the ordeal wasn't yet over. In the confusion of the fight, he watched the Mexican marauders strip the dead cowboys of their clothing and concluded that the only way to survive was to beat them to it.

So Byers, by now shot through the arm and the stomach, ripped off his clothes, removing even his ring, and buried his face in the dirt as if dead. The ploy worked. Most of the bandits passed him over — except one, who rode past Byers firing several shots at the "body."

"One [bullet] grazed my head, and the others striking at my side, throwing dirt over me," Byers told the *Nugget*. "They stripped the bodies, cut open the valises, took all the horses and saddles and in fact everything they could, possibly getting altogether, including money, $2,000."

Later, Byers managed to leap aboard Old Man Clanton's chuck wagon and race to Tombstone, where he recounted the horrible tale to a shocked populace.

Within hours, heavily-armed citizens converged on Guadalupe Canyon seeking swift revenge. The Tombstone posse included Clanton's three sons — Phin, Ike, and Billy — and one-time justice of the peace Mike Gray, Dixie Lee's father. A band of ranchers from Animas Valley took off in pursuit of the culprits from the New Mexico side.

The posses came upon a grisly scene — five bodies lying naked where they fell. They hadn't been mutilated, meaning that the attackers were probably not Apache, as some first speculated. But survivor Byers left no doubt about the identities of the gunmen — they were Mexican troops led by a Captain Carillo from Fronteras, Sonora.

That contention prevailed, and newspapers such as the *Arizona Weekly Star* and the *Tombstone Nugget* were soon reporting as fact the guilt of Carillo's troops.

But some never bought that story, choosing instead to posit widely varying and sometimes outrageous explanations. One of the wildest held that the men behind the guns in Guadalupe Canyon were named Earp. No blood could spill on Cochise County soil in the early 1880s without someone attributing it to the fabled Earps of Tombstone.

This theory had few serious adherents, but it was based on a plausible premise — that the Earps set out to murder their archenemy Clanton, thus ending the long-standing feud between the two families.

Still others suspected that the massacre was connected to Jim Crane's alleged involvement in the deadly Benson stagecoach holdup. After all, his two accomplices — Billy Leonard and Harry Head — had already been gunned down in another holdup attempt in Owl City, New Mexico, leaving "Slim Jim" as the gang's last survivor. Could he have been the target of the attackers?

But the most likely explanation is that the massacre was revenge against Clanton for leading a band of killers in an attack on a Mexican smugglers' train. The ambush of the Mexicans took place in early August 1881 in Skeleton Canyon, a pass in the Peloncillo Mountains at the southern end of the San Simon Valley.

According to the *Journal of Arizona History*, Clanton's raiding party of 20 cowboys, including the notorious bad man Curly Bill Brocius, made off with about $4,000 in Mexican coin, silver bullion, mescal, horses, and cattle.

Published estimates of the number of Mexicans killed in the raid begin at three and go up to 19. The *Tombstone Nugget* of August 5, 1881, reported that the shooting erupted when the party of 16 Mexicans stopped at a curve in the road to eat breakfast.

"While busily engaged preparing their tortillas, they were saluted with the music of 20 rifles fired by cowboys who lay in ambush awaiting them," the *Nugget* wrote. "The Mexicans took this as an invitation to leave."

In his book, *Doc Holliday*, writer John Myers Myers states that shortly after the Skeleton Canyon butchery, outlaws Johnny Ringo and Curly Bill led a cattle raid into Sonora, during which 14 Mexican ranch hands were shot dead and those caught alive were tortured.

"Old Man Clanton wasn't in on that particular deal, but he contracted to handle the stock which the raiders drove north," wrote Myers. "That turned out to be a mistake."

Myers' contention is that Clanton's role in these two incidents led to his death in Guadalupe Canyon. The *Journal of Arizona History* concurred that the motive of the attackers probably was revenge, but traced it solely to the murders in Skeleton Canyon.

The *Journal* concluded that Captain Carillo was known to be scouting the Guadalupe Canyon area for a party of cowboys who "had been depredating on Mexican soil."

But on the issue of border violence among outlaws, by necessity a secretive bunch, the historical record is invariably fuzzy. Firm clues are few. Many have raised serious doubts that Clanton was anywhere near Skeleton Canyon the day of the attack. Others believe his outlaw activities have been generally overstated.

If true, that lays bare the most chilling prospect of all — that in his desire for revenge, Captain Carillo might have gotten the wrong man in Newman H. Clanton and cruelly killed four other innocents in the bargain on that terrible day in Guadalupe Canyon.

CHAPTER EIGHT

The Blood of the Hernandez Family

*On a hot summer night, a popular
Tucson shopkeeper and his wife
were brutally bludgeoned and
their throats slit as they slept.
Their blood led to the apprehension
of their murderers, and from there,
vigilantes dealt swift justice to the killers
of the Hernandez family.*

BY LEO W. BANKS

━━◆◆◆━━

J ESUS SAGUARIPA WAS A MURDERER WHO COULDN'T STAND BLOOD. He was the one who worked the knife against the throats of the two victims, and it got to him.

Later that night, he couldn't sleep. He was agitated, pacing. He got up and lit a candle and inspected his hands and feet under the flame. He demanded a clean set of clothes.

His wife asked what was wrong, but he brushed her off. He left their shack and walked a short distance to the banks of the Santa Cruz River to wash himself again.

It was the second time he'd bathed that morning, Thursday, August 7, 1873. He returned wearing the fresh clothes, but failed to bring back the soiled ones. Still, he couldn't get rid of the blood.

When lawmen came for him the next day, Saguaripa swore to his innocence. But Pima County Sheriff W.S. Oury parted the suspect's toes with a pocketknife and scraped off a fleck of dried blood.

PIMA COUNTY SHERIFF WILLIAM S. OURY
MADE THE ARRESTS FOR THE HERNANDEZ MURDERS.

The crack-up was coming. At the murder scene, Saguaripa weakened further when his feet and hands were shown to match some of the bloody prints the killers had left behind. It was only a matter of time.

Saguaripa was taken to view the bodies. As the faces of Vicente and Librada Hernandez were uncovered, the trembling young man was asked if he would swear on the holy cross that he had nothing to do with the deaths of the couple before him.

Saguaripa shuddered in his guilt and said: "For God's sake, lead me away. I will tell you everything."

It was a grim tale. Saguaripa and two accomplices killed Vicente and Librada Hernandez as they slept on the floor of their adobe home on Tucson's Convent Street, south of present-day downtown.

After going for a stroll along the Santa Cruz, the couple

decided to leave the rear door of their home open as they slept, hoping for a breeze.

Their home also housed the Hernandez family business, a general store and pawnshop called Las Piedras Negras, "the black stones."

About midnight on Wednesday, August 6, the three killers crept in the open back door intending to commit robbery. How that changed into a gruesome double murder has never been established.

The group's ringleader was Leonardo Cordova. He was half-Opata Indian and half-Mexican, about 32 years old, a powerful man with remarkably small hands and feet.

He took up a large mesquite club and bludgeoned the sleeping couple. The weapon's knotted end was found matted with blood and hair. Then Saguaripa used a knife to sever their jugular veins, ensuring death.

As this grim business was going on, 26-year-old Clemente Lopez stood lookout. When they were done killing, the men ransacked the Hernandezes' trunks and showcases hunting for valuables. Their meager take emphasized the pointlessness of their work — some pistols, a saddle and bridle, a watch, and $37 in cash.

The bodies were discovered about 11 A.M. on Thursday when a woman, who couldn't get a response at the front door, went around to the back and found the trail of bloody footprints.

Soon Las Piedras Negras was swarming with lawmen and outraged citizens, including merchant William Zeckendorf, the community's most prominent figure. He had known Vicente and Librada years earlier in New Mexico and remained their good and generous friend when they reunited in Arizona.

Zeckendorf's anger at the murders was felt throughout Tucson, and it intensified when word spread that Librada had been several months pregnant.

This additional outrage led to the formation that same morning of a 30-member committee of public safety, with Zeckendorf as its leader. The Hernandezes were well liked,

JOHN SPRING, RESPECTED TUCSON SCHOOLTEACHER AND
U.S. ARMY VETERAN, WAS ONE OF 30 VIGILANTES
WHO AVENGED THE HERNANDEZES.

and more than one committee member had counted the couple as personal friends.

In a 1903 account of the murders and their aftermath, Tucsonan John Spring wrote that the committee hired a posse to find the men responsible and pledged themselves to stand by each other, "whatever might be the outcome of the business."

What Spring, a schoolteacher and committee member, was politely describing amounted to vigilante justice.

"It was tacitly understood," he wrote, "that if the assassins were apprehended, the judicial authorities would for [the] time being be deprived of their power and the criminals would be . . . tried and sentenced by the people, which said committee represented."

Everyone understood that the duly sworn officers of the law had been stripped of their power and that the vigilantes were calling the shots.

TUCSON MERCHANT WILLIAM ZECKENDORF,
SHOWN HERE WITH HIS FAMILY, LED THE
"COMMITTEE OF PUBLIC SAFETY."

The murders proved remarkably easy to solve, and it was the blood that did it. After splitting the money with his confederates, Saguaripa returned to his shack, apparently unaware that the bills held his bloody fingerprints. Later that day, Saguaripa's wife gave a neighboring washerwoman a few of the tainted bills and asked her to pick up some groceries on her trip to town. The washerwoman, apparently one of the few citizens unaware of the events at Las Piedras Negras the night before, went innocently about her shopping and attempted to pay with the bloody bills.

"The woman was detained in conversation by the grocery man," Spring wrote, "while his boy went for Mr. Zeckendorf. He was promptly on hand and requested the woman to accompany him to his office on Main Street where he managed to hide the sheriff behind a small partition wall."

Zeckendorf engaged the woman in innocent small talk, then loosed her tongue further with a cup of mescal. She gabbily revealed the source of the bills, giving Zeckendorf the name of the handsome, light-complected young man named Jesus Saguaripa.

By 10 P.M. that night, the three were in custody, and the stolen property was recovered under some brush on the road to Warren's Mill. It all happened so quickly that Vicente Hernandez's silver watch was still ticking. The men of Zeckendorf's committee advised the prisoners, who were shackled in chains in the jail, to prepare for death by hanging.

It was a fate preordained by events of the previous 18 months, during which three murderers saw their cases either postponed or dismissed by what much of the population considered legal trickery.

An angry and vengeful mood had been building in the populace, prompting a warning from the (Tucson) *Arizona Citizen* of March 29, 1873:

"The only comment we need make on these cases is to state that pretty good men are again talking of the necessity of a vigilance committee to administer that punishment which the law says shall be [but is not] for the terrible crime of murder.

"Murder upon murder is committed in Arizona and yet not one murderer has ever been punished as the law directs."

Zeckendorf and his men would make sure that it would be different this time.

The Hernandez funeral on the morning of Friday, August 8, was the biggest Tucson had yet seen. Every business in town was closed and the streets were empty, except around St. Augustine's Cathedral, where the mourners gathered with fitting solemnity.

As the procession bearing the remains of the murdered couple was winding its way to the cemetery, 10 of Zeckendorf's vigilantes were building a makeshift gallows in front of the courthouse.

They planted four strong posts, forked at the top, with a piece of timber placed in the grooves. Four ropes, not just three, dangled from this stout cross beam.

It had been decided that three lynchings would not be enough. To show the people's resolve, the committee decided that John Willis, a convicted murderer still fighting his death sentence by legal means, would also die that morning.

After seeing Vicente and Librada Hernandez to their rest, the crowd made an orderly march to the courthouse plaza with the intention, in the *Citizen's* words, of "closing the earthly careers of the three confessed murderers."

The paper continued: "It appeared to the careful observer as if the interment of the bodies of the murdered man and woman would be incomplete without placing those who so brutally killed them, beyond the possibility of repeating the offense."

The public's desire to kill was overwhelming, and none of the bearers of law who could stop it rose to do so. In a retrospective article published 19 years after the fact, the *Arizona Weekly Enterprise* wrote sarcastically about the whereabouts of two of Tucson's leading authorities that day.

Judge John Titus, chief justice of the territory, was said by the *Enterprise* to be a great admirer of Spanish architecture, and he happened to choose that day, Friday, August 8, to visit San Xavier, the old church built between the mid-1770s and about 1797.

"The judge thought an outing might be conducive to a better appetite for dinner and left," wrote the *Enterprise*.

As for the sheriff, the paper wrote that he was at home sick, "having partaken of too much watermelon the night before."

Zeckendorf mounted a platform on the plaza and gave an impassioned speech about the sorry state of crime and punishment in the territory, then recited the overwhelming evidence against the accused men.

"I ask you, the people of Tucson here assembled," he boomed, "what punishment have the murderers deserved?"

"Death!" was the shouted response.

A similar oratory was delivered in Spanish, and the impassioned response was the same. The only voice of protest came from Milton B. Duffield, a former U.S. marshal for Arizona. But the crowd refused to heed Duffield's objections, and he was quickly bound by his hands and feet and spirited away.

At Zeckendorf's command, two wagons were drawn up under the gallows and the four men were hoisted aboard.

Some observers noticed that Willis needed to be propped up, leading to speculation that he'd resisted efforts of the vigilantes to remove him from the jail and was already dead when lifted onto the wagon.

Cordova won a brief delay when he was granted permission to speak his last words. As he began to list his previous crimes, including a murder at Yuma and another in the Salt River country, one of the throng cut him off, shouting that they'd better get on with it because troops were on the way from Ft. Lowell. Cordova's desire to unburden himself abruptly ended when the wagons were jerked away.

Nothing of the agony of the four men was visible, wrote schoolteacher John Spring, "except a few shivers that ran through their bodies."

Then he added: "Perfect stillness reigned over the plaza, where fully 2,000 people were assembled. The only sound faintly perceptible was a humming as of many bees; it proceeded from the Mexican women reading under their breath the Mass for the dead."

Pima County Coroner Solomon Warner made his inquest while the bodies were still swinging. Using all the expertise that science and experience could offer, he concluded that the men came to their deaths by hanging, "committed by the people of Tucson, en masse."

"No regrets are expressed as far as we have heard," wrote the *Citizen* a week later. "The mind of the people was never more tranquil."

But what of the mind of Jesus Saguaripa, the murderer spooked by blood? Was his mind finally tranquil, too?

The Two Worlds
of Cesario Lucero

Cesario Lucero, one of the best lawmen
of the borderlands, tracked bad men
all over Arizona and deep into Mexico.
But when Mexican train robber Manuel Robles
escaped a shootout with Lucero and
other lawmen, the hunter became
the hunted and nowhere
in Arizona or Mexico was safe.

BY LEO W. BANKS

━━━━◆◆◆━━━━

ESARIO LUCERO LIVED IN A WORLD OF SHADOWS. HIS TER-
ritory was the border between Mexico and Arizona, and
his time was the 1880s. A tracker for the Cochise County
Sheriff's office, he probably was as valuable in putting criminals
in chains as any of the great marshals upon whom history has
bestowed fame.

In this violent border world, a place of two languages,
two cultures, and serpentine allegiances, Lucero performed
brilliantly and anonymously. He was never quoted, never fea-
tured, and rarely credited.

Only toward the end of his life was he praised as the
best Mexican detective in the Southwest. But by then, the
criminals he hunted, his own countrymen, had marked him
as a traitor deserving assassination.

Recorded facts about Lucero's personal life are few. He
is not listed in the 1880 U.S. Census for Arizona, or in the Great
Register of Cochise County, so the date and place of his birth are

unknown, although the latter was probably Mexico. Whether he was married and had children is also a mystery today. But his character is well-defined by his work as a tracker.

Lucero was called upon by Cochise County Sheriff Jerome L. Ward after the Bisbee Massacre of 1883. The trouble started on a cold December day when five gunmen botched their attempt to rob the Goldwater and Castaneda Mercantile on Main Street. Five bystanders, including a pregnant woman and her unborn baby, died as a result of the shooting that accompanied the bandits' getaway. Two of them — W.E. "Bill" Delaney and Dan Dowd — rode toward John Slaughter's ranch near Douglas, then picked up the smuggler's route south into Mexico.

Deputy Billy Daniels and Lucero reportedly trailed them to the old Spanish town of Bavispe, Sonora. The fugitives separated there and so did the lawmen, with Daniels going after Dowd and Lucero taking Delaney.

It was perilous work. Delaney was a hot-tempered 27-year-old from Pennsylvania, considered the most dangerous man in the gang. Writer Harriet Hankin, in a typescript about the massacre on file at the Arizona Historical Society, described him as "a dark, agile man of medium height, vicious and aggressive in disposition, reputed to be a dead shot with a rifle."

Delaney was on the run from a murder charge in Graham County at the time. He'd shot a man through the heart for interfering in his quarrel with a Mexican woman.

After separating from Dowd, Hankin wrote, Delaney "simply disappeared, and for a while no trace of him could be found."

But Lucero never lost the scent. He dogged his prey deep into Sonora over several hundred miles. He passed out handbills containing a description of Delaney in the villages and to Mexican police.

His diligence paid off when, according to Hankin, Delaney's "ugly temper overcame his discretion," and he got involved in a saloon brawl in Minas Prietas, near Hermosillo. Mexican police thought they recognized him from the handbills and took him in. He was the last of the robbers arrested, and all of them died at the end of a rope.

Even though Delaney's capture might never have occurred without Lucero's knowledge of Mexico, the deputy was largely absent from the congratulatory press accounts of the day. He remained in the background on other occasions as well.

On May 11, 1888, several masked men held up a train at Agua Zarca, Mexico, 12 miles south of Nogales. They coldly killed the conductor and brakeman and wounded several others before fleeing into Arizona.

One of them, an Anglo named J.J. Taylor, was arrested within hours after investigators found his hat at the scene. The remaining four, all Mexicans, vanished somewhere in southern Arizona.

Over the next month, Cochise County Sheriff John Slaughter pursued the murderers from Fairbank to Willcox, Clifton, and Tombstone. It was an arduous and frustrating chase. The men kept moving, taking and shedding names like clothing, and using friends, family, and their knowledge of the terrain to stay ahead of the law.

Early in June, after spending a night in Tombstone, two of the robbers, Manuel Robles and another known in some accounts as Nievas Deron, left for the Whetstone Mountains, west of town. Robles' brother, Guadalupe, worked there as a woodcutter.

Lucero, along with Slaughter and Deputy Burt Alvord, followed close behind, and came upon the fugitives at Mescal Springs at dawn the morning of June 6.

"When within some 80 yards of the camp," reported the (Tucson) *Arizona Daily Star*, "they all removed their shoes and proceeded in their stocking feet. When they came to the men they found them lying by a fire wrapped in their blankets. The sheriff ordered them to throw up their hands and surrender."

But the fugitives woke up firing. So did Guadalupe Robles, whose only crime was his blood relation to Manuel.

**DOWD AND HIS GANG WERE BURIED
AT TOMBSTONE'S BOOT HILL.**

The *Star* reported that Guadalupe was killed almost instantly, "with a Colt .45 in his hand, full cocked, ready to shoot."

Nievas Deron fled some 40 feet up a nearby hill, dodging behind trees and firing as he ran. But Slaughter brought him down with a fatal charge of buckshot. Manuel Robles ran down French Joe Canyon with Lucero, Alvord, and Slaughter at his back.

"It was a running fight," the *Star* reported, "and as Alvord was without shoes, the Mexican escaped." But not before he'd been hit by two rounds from Slaughter's shotgun and a third from Alvord's Winchester rifle.

Robles fell after each wound, but kept getting back up and running. The lawmen trailed him for more than two miles by the blood that flowed from his wounds, but he got away. The sheriff boasted that Robles wouldn't live long.

Much of the credit for the successful routing of the murderers went to Slaughter.

"It is not every county that has a sheriff brave enough to walk over the mountains in his bare feet to capture desperate criminals," reported the *Tombstone Prospector*.

But Lucero, whose knowledge of the back alleys of Mexican Tombstone was key to the pursuit, finally got some recognition, too, when the *Prospector* paid tribute to his "coolness, bravery and shrewdness" in the shoot-out.

Unfortunately for Lucero, Slaughter was wrong in predicting Manuel Robles' death. The killer survived his wounds, reunited with two more of the gang — Fredrico Acuna and Geronimo Miranda (or Baldon, depending on the account) — and swore revenge against Lucero.

At a dance at Fort Thomas, late in July, Lucero was assaulted by a friend of the men killed in the Whetstone Mountain fight. The *Prospector* reported that Cipriano Lopez approached the tracker and asked if Lucero was his name.

When the answer came back yes, Lopez growled, "You killed one of my friends and I'm going to kill you." He drew a knife and lunged at Lucero, but was knocked down by a bystander and arrested.

Lucero was not hurt, but the incident demonstrated the contempt in which he was held by other Mexicans for merely doing his job.

"It was indicative of the price paid by Mexican and Indian peace officers in the Southwest when they remained loyal to their oath of office," says historian Lori Davisson, who has researched the careers of numerous territorial lawmen, including Lucero.

With his ability to read the whispers and rumors that ran through the Mexican neighborhoods and towns on both sides of the border, Lucero surely knew he was a marked man. But he pushed the threats aside and stayed on the trail of the Agua

Zarca killers. It turned out that they were tracking him, too.

Early in August, Lucero departed Tombstone for the Mescal Ranch in the San Jose Mountains, a short distance south of the Arizona border. The *Arizona Weekly Citizen* reported that he went "with the idea of entering into the business of buying and selling mescal [a liquor made from agaves]."

Lucero was unaware that Manuel, in company with Acuna and Miranda, was watching. The *Citizen* gave the following account of what happened on Sunday, August 12, 1888:

"Manuel was seen on Saturday night near the Mescal Ranch. On Sunday morning, Lucero went to the creek which runs through the ranch about two hundred yards distant from the house. He went unarmed, leaving his rifle at the house, not expecting any danger.

"After washing himself he sauntered back, but had proceeded but a few yards when the crack of a rifle shot was heard, quickly followed by a second report, and Lucero was seen to fall in his tracks.

"Two men were seen to run away after convincing themselves that their victim was dead. They were recognized as Fredrico [Acuna] and Geronimo [Miranda], two of the train robbers, for which a large reward is offered, but up to the present time have evaded arrest or a more merited death.

"On examination of the body of the murdered man, it was found that he had received two bullet wounds, both in the head. Death must have been instantaneous."

A somewhat different version was told in *The Southwest of John H. Slaughter*, by Allen A. Erwin. He wrote that Lucero was tracking Geronimo Miranda that day, on orders from Slaughter.

Erwin also recounted, in what might be more folklore than fact, that when Miranda approached Lucero at the stream, the outlaw was "smiling as if greeting a brother" when he said, "I understand you are after me." Lucero was shot dead before he could reply.

In death, Lucero received the full acclaim that eluded

him in life. The *Tombstone Epitaph* for August 25 wrote that "few better, and no braver, man than Cesario Lucero ever met death at the hands of cowardly assassins."

Public demands for retribution against Miranda became intense, even though it was never firmly established that he was the actual triggerman. He proved a formidable adversary for Slaughter, who chased him for two more years without success.

Geronimo Miranda finally met his end, in June 1891, when he was gunned down by ranchers near Benson after stealing some horses. Two years after that, a bizarre story appeared in the *San Francisco Examiner*, saying that the bandit's head had been cut off and preserved by his killer, identified only as Gray, in an effort to claim the reward. When that proved futile, Gray buried the head. It was later dug up, according to the story, by a surveyor from Oakland working in Arizona for Southern Pacific. The surveyor shipped it to a San Francisco horse stable, where the stable men used the grisly artifact to terrify neighborhood children.

But Miranda's death amounted to small vengeance. Acuna and Robles, the others involved in Lucero's assassination, escaped Slaughter's reach and were never heard from again.

As for Lucero, it was said that he had been warned repeatedly against exposing himself to the dangers of riding alone through the countryside. But the tracker always replied that he feared nothing.

He still rests where he fell at Mescal Ranch, a dedicated lawman who suffered the bitterness and hatred of his own people.

CHAPTER TEN

In Pursuit
of Fleming Parker

*A well-liked cowboy, Fleming "Jim" Parker,
robbed a train and then led Sheriff George
Ruffner on a long-distance manhunt across
northern Arizona. Captured and confined to the
Yavapai County jail, Parker killed a man during
his escape and fled on Ruffner's favorite horse.
Parker's flight and tricks on the trail are
legendary as is Ruffner's tenacious pursuit that
finally brought Parker to the end of his rope.*

BY LEO W. BANKS

=⇒◆⇐=

FOR 16 MONTHS IN 1897 AND 1898, NORTHERN ARIZONA watched with keen intensity as a gripping story of good and evil played out before its eyes.

On one side was a train robber turned killer named Fleming Parker, a cagey desperado who saved his most daring exploits for moments when all seemed lost. On the other was Yavapai County Sheriff George Ruffner, a peace officer whose heroic determination brought Parker to final justice after one of the longest and most frustrating manhunts in territorial history.

The tale began to unfold on a bitter, cold February night eight miles east of Peach Springs. William Daze, a veteran engineer on the Santa Fe railroad, was steaming through a rocky canyon when he spotted a waving lantern in the dark distance, a common sign of trouble on the line.

But when Daze and his fireman stopped the train to help,

they were met by a man wearing a black mask and brandishing a pistol at them.

It was Fleming Parker. He commanded the men to jump down and uncouple the express and mail cars from the remainder of the train. To emphasize his order, Parker fired two shots near the fireman's feet, saying: "If you don't hurry up, I will shoot off your heels."

Even before hearing the shots, a railroad employee named Summers jumped from the back of the express car with his Colt .45 drawn and quickly encountered one of the robbers. The ensuing gunfight was entirely one-sided, involving two rounds from Summers' gun — the first striking the masked figure just above the heart, the second in the left eye. The bandit, whose name was never revealed, was dead before he fell by the tracks.

Summers and a colleague failed in their efforts to board the front section of the train, which by that time was already steaming forward. The robbers' plan was to reach Nelson Siding, two miles ahead, and plunder the express car of its riches.

But for reasons never fully explained, the dynamite the men carried to blow the express safe wasn't put to use, and the Peach Springs heist ended in failure. The hunt for Parker and his accomplices — identified by most sources as Abe Thompson and "Kid" Marvin — began almost immediately.

The pursuit was marked by running gun battles on rugged terrain near the Grand Canyon. Parker, separated from his confederates, managed to elude the law for eight freezing days, and his capture was largely a matter of luck. One of Ruffner's deputies and his Indian trackers stumbled upon the outlaw in Diamond Canyon and took him into custody. The posse then set up camp to wait for Ruffner, who had dropped back to butcher a cow.

The delay gave Parker an opportunity to demonstrate his resourcefulness. At the first lapse in the posse's concentration, he sprang to his feet and grabbed a Winchester, sending a bullet whizzing past the terrified deputy's ear as he bolted from the scene.

The Indians ran, too, and Parker was again a fugitive. But his freedom was short-lived. The following morning, Ruffner and two other men were tracking along Diamond Creek when they spotted Parker coming toward them, and they hid. As Parker drew up alongside Ruffner's hiding place, the sheriff revealed himself and barked his order: "Hands up!" Parker did so, and Ruffner brought him to Prescott with the fanfare due an outlaw worthy of $4,000 in reward money.

Parker's accomplices, Abe Thompson and "Kid" Marvin, were arrested. Thompson was convicted and served time at Yuma Territorial Prison. Marvin likely also met the same fate, although under what name is uncertain.

Facts about the captured train robber soon hung on the lips of every citizen of Prescott. Fleming Parker, commonly known as Jim, had been a highly regarded cowboy and horse breaker in the Flagstaff area for several years. Many knew him as a participant in a bronco-busting tournament in Prescott in July 1895.

A native of Tulare County, Califorña, Parker had drifted to Arizona after doing a five-year hitch at San Quentin for stealing grain. He was said to ride with a gang of horse- and cattle-thieving cowboys who made their headquarters in a place called Robber's Roost, near the Arizona-Utah border.

The (Prescott) *Arizona Weekly Journal-Miner* described Parker as "below average in stature, somewhat heavyset, of a determined expression and with a light mustache. His physical bearing, in short, is of a typical wild and woolly cowboy."

With Parker in custody awaiting trial, and Ruffner praised by the *Journal-Miner* as a man of "sagacity and courage" who was so dedicated he never bothered to sleep while hunting outlaws, the episode seemed over.

But Parker's hold on the public's attention was only beginning. Four months later, he and two other prisoners engineered a break from the Yavapai County Jail, which the

Journal-Miner called "one of the most daring ever attempted by desperate men."

It began about 1 P.M. on Sunday, May 9, when a Mexican prisoner, whose identity was never made known, asked jailer Bob Meador if he could refill his water bucket.

As soon as the cell door clanged open, the Mexican attacked Meador, finally ripping the key from the jailer's grasp and slashing his scalp with it. This disabled Meador, allowing Parker and a forger named L.C. Miller to dash out of the cell.

In the adjoining room, Parker grabbed a shotgun, a Winchester rifle, and a six-shooter. He exited into a corridor just as Assistant County Attorney Lee Norris, answering Meador's cries for help, was coming down the stairs from the courthouse above. When he spotted the mayhem, Norris turned and attempted to flee back up the stairs. Parker's response was to fire a shotgun blast into the lawyer's back.

The three men fled to a stable next door owned by Sheriff Ruffner. They grabbed two getaway horses, with Miller and the Mexican riding together, and galloped out of Prescott past townsfolk so shocked by the goings-on that they stood slack-jawed, unable to respond.

A quickly formed posse engaged two of the fugitives near Lynx Creek about 5 P.M. that same day. However, the Mexican, evidently splitting from the gang shortly after leaving Prescott, was nowhere in sight. He was never heard from again.

Miller's horse was shot from under him in the gunplay, so Parker pulled him onto the back of his own horse and the two made a dramatic getaway.

But their association didn't last long. Miller, apparently wanting no more of Parker's close calls, split for his sister's house in Jerome and was captured two days later.

That meant Parker was riding alone. Again, Ruffner was on his tail, more determined than ever, as the horse Parker had stolen from the stable was Ruffner's prized white mount Sure Shot, said to be the fastest horse in Prescott.

On top of that came news that 28-year-old Lee Norris,

the attorney shot during the jail break, had died from his wounds. His death meant that the Peach Springs train robber had jumped the line to murderer, and it marked the start of Fleming Parker's demonization.

In a siren call of journalistic excess, the Prescott press called Norris' killing "one of the most foul murders that has ever blotted the pages of the history of our territory." The papers also carried dire warnings of Parker's promise "to die happy if he can only kill Sheriff Ruffner."

Later, as the second manhunt stretched into weeks, wild rumors of Parker's dark deeds filtered back to town. The most outrageous, utterly without foundation, was that Sure Shot had been discovered dead on the trail, his throat slashed.

But of one matter there was little doubt: Parker's extraordinary cunning in evading the force of lawmen at his heels.

His tricks included periodically changing his horse's shoes, tacking them on backwards, and riding in a wide circle while making sure to cross his own trail. He also removed his horse's shoes altogether and rode among a band of range horses, further confounding Ruffner's men.

Parker's knowledge of the land from his cowboy days, and his numerous friends still working the ranges there, proved invaluable in securing fresh horses, food, and ammunition.

At times the law was so close that Ruffner's Indian trackers quit the chase, believing capture was imminent. But each time, Parker seemed to sense their presence and jump ahead. Some have written that he neutralized the bloodhounds at his back by sprinkling the trail with cayenne pepper, leaving the dogs gasping, unable to go on.

After three long weeks on the run, Parker stopped at a trading post north of Flagstaff for food. Owner S.S. Preston recognized the bandit and assembled an impromptu posse of 10 Navajos to go after him.

For all the huffing and puffing involved in the hunt, the capture was remarkably simple. They found Parker at his campsite, revealed their superior numbers, and allowed the fugitive to make his own decision. He wisely gave up.

The train bearing Parker and Miller, who was picked up at the Flagstaff jail, arrived in Prescott on June 1. A huge crowd waited at the station to greet Parker, now considered the worst bad man in the territory.

Fearing the mob might take its own justice, authorities stopped the train short of the depot and spirited the two men to the courthouse in carriages. The crowd got wind of the ruse and marched to the courthouse, where a terrified Miller declared: "My God, they're coming to hang us!"

Parker let out a volley of profanity at his partner, whom he considered a coward.

"You can't die but once anyway," he reportedly told Miller.

Every remark that Parker made was duly reported in the Prescott newspapers. And his every court appearance drew mobs of ghoulish gawkers, each hoping to glimpse the demon himself.

Parker's public comments did nothing to dispel his devilish image. He said he regretted not getting the opportunity to shoot Ruffner and predicted that he wouldn't be present at the courthouse when his trial date came, nor would Ruffner see him hang.

Wrong on both counts. Parker was quickly found guilty of murder and sentenced to hang, although the execution was delayed by a year of legal wrangling.

For most of execution eve, Ruffner stayed at the side of the man he so eagerly had sought for so many hard days. The steel gaze of the relentless peace officer must have softened a bit as he listened to Parker talk about his life, which now was so near its close.

Ruffner even allowed Parker to sip some whiskey until 4 A.M., when the condemned man fell into a fitful sleep.

Next morning, June 3, 1898, Parker ate a last breakfast, consulted with a priest, put on his execution clothes — a shiny black suit and pressed white shirt — and listened as Ruffner read the death warrant.

FLEMING "JIM" PARKER AWAITING HIS EXECUTION.

The first break in Parker's cool demeanor came when he was led outside and got his first look at the scaffolding that was about to transport him from, in the *Journal-Miner's* words, "the environment of this earth into the great unknown beyond."

With his composure regained and a big crowd watching, Parker mounted the scaffolding and steadied his feet on the platform.

"Hello, Jack!" he called to a friend. "How are they breaking?"

Parker was asked if he'd like to make a last comment: "I have not much to say. I claim that I am getting something that ain't due me, but I guess that every man that is about to be hanged says the same thing, so that don't cut no figure. Whenever the people say that I must go, I am one who can go and make no kick."

The man who gained notoriety riding the sheriff's white horse was calm again as he shook hands around the platform and asked that a message be given to his friends back in the jail.

"Tell the boys I died game and like a man," he said.

As Ruffner's trembling hand inched toward the trip lever, Parker cautioned him, "Don't get excited."

It might've been that the nervous sheriff was thinking of one of Parker's sisters, living in Utah, who was so distraught at the thought of her brother's impending execution that she died.

Or maybe he was thinking of Sadie Baker in Los Angeles, another of Parker's sisters, who penned emotional letters to Ruffner pleading for her brother's life.

In one correspondence, Baker wrote of her criminal brother: "Poor fellow, he has been turned out in the world ever since he was 12 years old. Mother and Father both died when we were very young, and we just had to do the best we could and poor Flem, he never had any raising like other boys. . . . It is so hard for me to give him up that way. . . . He is in my mind the last thing at night and the first thing in the morning and I dream about him."

Perhaps the good sheriff knew, as he flipped the lever and heard the awful crash of that trapdoor, that to at least two people on this earth, Fleming Parker hadn't been a demon at all.

CHAPTER ELEVEN

The Wham Pay Wagon Robbery

*In a fierce firefight, at least seven men
ambushed two Army pay wagons carrying
almost $29,000 in gold and silver coins. Eight
of the 11 black soldiers under the command of
Maj. Joseph Washington Wham were wounded
before retreating. The investigation of the
robbery, the arrest of prominent
Mormon ranchers, and the well-publicized trial
yielded bizarre twists and turns that made the
Wham pay wagon robbery among the most
celebrated crimes in Arizona history.*

BY LEO W. BANKS

⟾◆⟾

THE TWO U.S. ARMY PAY WAGONS AND THEIR ARMED ES-
cort, dusty and hot under the Arizona afternoon sun,
dipped into a horseshoe-shaped gorge made cool by the
waters of Cottonwood Creek. As the road curved and began
its ascent, troopers of the 24th Infantry and the 10th Cavalry,
two famed black Army units, came upon a boulder obstruct-
ing their course. The men coaxed their mules to a stop and
jumped down to inspect the blockage.

It was about 1 P.M. on May 11, 1889, and one of the most
celebrated and scandalous crimes in Arizona Territory's history was about to unfold.

The wagons had left Fort Grant that morning headed for

**A 20TH-CENTURY RE-ENACTMENT
OF THE WHAM ROBBERY, PHOTOGRAPHED
AT THE AMBUSH SCENE.**

Fort Thomas, 46 miles to the north at the southern boundary of the San Carlos Indian Reservation. In the boot of the lead wagon was a chest containing nearly $28,500 in payroll money, most of that in gold coins. The mission was under the command of Major Joseph Washington Wham (rhymes with "bomb"), accompanied by an escort of 11 soldiers.

Even with such treasure on board, the boulder created no suspicions. It appeared to the troopers that the rock had simply fallen there from farther up the hill. But on closer inspection, Pvt. Julius Harrison spotted something that sent a chill up his spine. The boulder was wedged in place by dirt and small stones. That meant someone had secured it there deliberately. And that meant ambush.

The shooting erupted just after Harrison cried, "Boys, that rock was rolled here by human hands!" The first volley left three soldiers wounded and the same number of mules dead in their harnesses.

Wham's and his escort's responses were slowed by their surprise. Still, the troops managed to heat up their carbines, aiming at the puffs of gunsmoke that curled above the high rocks.

"Get out, you black sons-of-bitches!" one of the attacking riflemen shouted as the firing became general. Shots rained down on paymaster Wham and his escort for longer than 30 minutes.

A later inspection of the ambush site turned up some 200 spent shells and several rock forts that investigators estimated took 15 men at least two days to build. Poking out from between the rocks of these entrenchments were hollowed mescal stalks — the pith had been extracted to give them the appearance of gun barrels, a purely psychological ploy that elevated the art of ambush to a new height.

By the time Wham and his men, all of whom fought bravely, abandoned the gold to the robbers, eight of the 11 soldiers were wounded.

The Wham Robbery, as it came to be called, was an instant sensation, grabbing press attention around the Southwest.

Charges were eventually filed against seven men, most of them upstanding Mormon ranchers from Pima, a Graham County community settled by Mormons in 1879. Gilbert Webb and his son, Wilfred; brothers Lyman and Warren Follett; Thomas Lamb; and David Rogers were tried along with Marcus Cunningham, the only non-Mormon in the group. Some accounts name Ed Follett, brother of Lyman and Warren Follett, as a defendant. Although he was arrested for the robbery, the charges against him were eventually dropped, and Ed Follett never went to trial.

The heist and the subsequent trial in Tucson, which lasted 33 days and involved 165 witnesses, were in some ways historic. Observers believe the robbery was the West's only case of an attack by white men upon American troops, and two of the soldiers in Wham's escort were awarded Medals of Honor for their bravery.

One was Sgt. Benjamin Brown, who, according to an interview Wham gave to the *Arizona Weekly Citizen*, emptied his revolver, then "snatched a gun from one of his men and continued firing, but soon fell, shot through the arm and side."

The other honored soldier was Cpl. Isaiah Mays, who

**THE DEFENDANTS, SHOWN
WITH THEIR DEFENSE TEAM, WEATHERED MUCH
PUBLIC OUTCRY OVER THE WHAM CASE.**

crawled under an escort wagon and fired with his .38 revolver at the robbers' position in the rocks above. When he was out of ammunition, Mays ran up a hill opposite the robbers, reaching a rocky ledge where most of the soldiers were located. There, he borrowed a rifle and kept up the fire. Only when it became clear that the soldiers couldn't prevail did Mays retreat, helping several of his wounded comrades down the hill to safety.

But the Wham story was more than history; it was great public theater, serving up one strange twist after another. When investigators returned to the attack scene after the fight, they encountered a black woman who witnessed the ambush after being thrown from her horse and scrambling for cover.

Newspapers first reported that this witness, Frankie Campbell — also identified as Frankie Stratton — was a resident of a tiny town attached to Fort Thomas called Maxey, where she ran "a kind of money brokerage." Later reports made clear that the so-called brokerage was actually a gambling operation.

Campbell made her living running a game of monte for Army troops.

At the trial, wearing a yellow waist-shirt, a wine-colored skirt and a floppy hat decorated with roses over a velvet streamer, the flamboyant Campbell charmed the courtroom with her testimony.

Asked why she was travelling on the road that day, newspapers reported her as testifying, "Well . . . you see, me and my husband — he's one of the escorts — he and me runs a sort of a business . . . gambling. We open a little game of monte for the boys. I have to follow the Army cash . . . have to be close by on payday to collect our debts."

Cautioned by the judge to stop gesturing with her right hand, Campbell quipped that her left hand wasn't sworn.

Public sentiment against Major Wham was high for losing the payroll, most of it due to the widespread notion that the Civil War veteran was a coward. According to newspaper reports, when asked if Wham did any fighting, Campbell told the court, "Lord, no, suh. He run so fast you could'a played checkers on his coattails."

The full official transcript of the trial, uncovered by author Larry Ball at the National Archives in the early 1980s, contained no such quote in Campbell's testimony or from any of the other eyewitnesses. But the damning remark was widely reported as true, and it helped fuel a lasting antagonism toward Wham.

Campbell identified two of the defendants — Gilbert Webb and Thomas Lamb — as participants in the robbery. But many did not believe the lady gambler's testimony, speculating that Campbell was somehow a conspirator to the affair.

Another character on the Wham stage was William Ellison Beck, better known as Cyclone Bill, a nickname he acquired after bopping a man on the head with the leg of a cow. This prompted the victim to say that he thought he'd been hit by a cyclone.

Bill was an egomaniac who wanted to be known as a desperado, but didn't have the mettle to acquire the reputation

WILLIAM BREAKENRIDGE (LEFT), LATER KNOWN FOR HIS TOMBSTONE MEMOIRS, WAS CAUGHT UP IN THE TUMULT OF THE WHAM CASE FOR A WHILE.

honestly. He got a significant boost in the direction of infamy by fitting a description of one of the robbers. Investigators arrested him, and amid much fanfare, Deputy U.S. Marshal William Breakenridge brought Bill to Tucson in leg irons. When Cyclone Bill asked that the shackles be removed, Breakenridge responded that they were for Bill's protection. Bill didn't understand that, so Breakenridge explained: "If I take them off, you'll be damn fool enough to try to escape, and I'll have to kill you."

Wham was among those who said Bill was one of the robbers. However, Marshal W.K. Meade was forced to release Cyclone Bill when reliable witnesses testified that he was 85 miles from the robbery scene on May 11. But Cyclone Bill wouldn't go away. A month after his release, he was arrested again for carrying a concealed weapon. His ludicrous explanation was that Meade had made him a special deputy investigating the Wham Robbery.

William H. Barnes, the first judge in the case, proved

**WILLIAM H. BARNES WAS REPLACED
AS THE PRESIDING JUDGE.**

easier to sideline. In the early stages of the affair, he and Marshal
Meade openly feuded, raising fears that this would prejudice
the proceedings against the prosecution.

Members of the grand jury sent a telegram to the U.S.
attorney general, demanding that Barnes be removed. Hearing
this, Judge Barnes dismissed the jury, calling them "a band of
character assassins, unworthy to sit in any court of justice."
President Benjamin Harrison then stepped in and replaced
Barnes with Judge Richard E. Sloan of Florence.

According to a lengthy article on the case in the summer 1997 issue of the Journal of Arizona History, the trial's
outcome turned on several factors. One was the vehement bias
against the federal government prevalent among Territorial
citizens at that time. Another was a powerful undercurrent of
racism, fueled in part by the large number of ex-Confederates
who relocated to Arizona Territory after the Civil War.

**JUDGE RICHARD E. SLOAN CONSIDERED
AT LEAST SOME OF THE DEFENDANTS
TO BE OBVIOUSLY GUILTY.**

Even though several of the black soldiers testified and positively identified a number of the maskless robbers, who at times had been as close as 90 feet away, the jury chose to discount their statements.

Wham's testimony also hurt the prosecution, causing newspapers to joke that he was as bad a witness as he was a soldier. He identified two of the defendants, but the defense forced him to acknowledge that he couldn't be absolutely certain. That admission, coupled with his earlier mistake in naming Cyclone Bill, damaged Wham's credibility.

But the biggest blow to the government's case came when U.S. Attorney H.R. Jeffords scattered a fistful of gold coins on a table and asked Wham if these were among the ones stolen. Yes, the major said, asserting that he could tell by a certain discoloration they had. This implicated defendant Gilbert Webb, who had used those very coins to pay off several debts following the robbery.

That point, however, also was rendered moot when defense attorney Marcus Smith devised a brilliant rejoinder. As the proceedings broke for lunch, he hurried to a nearby bank and collected a number of similar coins, which he mixed among those Wham had identified.

When the trial resumed in the afternoon, Smith forced the beleaguered major to admit that he couldn't tell the two sets of coins apart. Despite these disasters and rampant local prejudices against the government and blacks, much of the public wanted a guilty verdict. Anti-Mormon sentiment also ran high, and it got a boost from the Territorial press, which took every opportunity to demonstrate its distaste for objectivity.

"Oh, what a tangled web we weave, when first we practice to deceive," wrote the *Arizona Daily Star*, as one family member after another marched to the stand with ironclad alibis for each of the defendants.

If the jurors were swayed, it was not by the religious bigots. They retired to their deliberation, ate supper, and returned in 33 minutes with a verdict of not guilty for all seven men.

The press went into apoplexy, sounding cries of perjury, bribery, and witness tampering and making dark pronouncements on the verdict's meaning. "We have made a covenant with death and with hell are we at agreement," boomed the *Star*, which published the names of the jurors in retaliation.

Even as the years wore on, the case lingered. Judge Sloan wrote a book in which he said that at least some of the defendants were obviously guilty. Cyclone Bill tried to pen his own memoir, but published sources indicate that he finished only a chapter.

Writer Owen Wister published a short story about the incident in *Harper's* magazine called "A Pilgrim on the Gila." Marcus Smith threatened libel action for his portrayal as an uncouth and loud-mouthed politician who bought votes. Yet Smith definitely benefitted from the publicity given the Wham case. His mid-day dash to the bank made him famous, and he was elected to the U.S. Senate following Arizona's admission to statehood in 1912.

In a 1937 interview, Wilfred Webb, then proprietor of a Graham County guest ranch, came tantalizingly close to admitting his complicity in the Wham Robbery. A Tucson contractor had donated to the Arizona Pioneers' Historical Society a chest believed to be the one that once held the Wham gold.

Webb inspected it and declared that it was not the same one. Asked how he could be so sure, Webb laughed and reminded the questioner that he had been one of the Wham Robbery defendants.

Then he said: "I've never denied or affirmed that I was in on it. In fact, over at my guest ranch, they make me tell the story of the robbery all the time because it gives the Easterners a thrill to be guests of a highway robber. I never was one to spoil a good story."

Webb said the courtroom coin fiasco and Wham's misidentification of Cyclone Bill forced the jury to acquit. "We all might have been guilty as hell, but those two things would have got us off," he said. The money was never recovered.

Major Wham, unable to shake the taint of cowardice, retired from the Army in 1901 and died seven years later. As for decorated soldiers Isaiah Mays and Benjamin Brown, they were heroes who met unfortunate ends. Brown, an alcoholic, retired from the Army in 1905 and died in 1910. Mays resigned from the Army in 1899 and spent much of the succeeding years living outside Fort Grant and attempting to get a military pension that was never granted. He died in Phoenix in 1925, penniless and alone at the state mental hospital.

The Power Brothers: Arizona's Largest Manhunt

At dawn, four lawmen approached a remote cabin to arrest the draft-dodging Power brothers and opened fire without identifying themselves. With their father lying mortally wounded, the brothers, still unaware it was the law staging the ambush, returned the fire, killing all but one of their attackers. Deputy Marshal Frank Haynes, the surviving lawman, rode off for reinforcements. Thus began the largest manhunt in Arizona history and it resulted in grievous miscarriages of justice.

B Y   D O N   D E D E R A

❦

KILLER OF A LAWMAN AND SENTENCED LIFER, TOM POWER demanded return of his good name. For decades a felon, he yearned to participate in an election. Just once . . . he hungered to be issued a ballot like everybody else, mark his X . . . and vote.

Tom was born, May 16, 1893, in the tiny farming settlement of Cliff, Grant County, New Mexico. After a sod roof collapsed and killed his mother, Tom's industrious but luckless father, Thomas Jefferson Power, Jr. (who went by Jeff), led his three children across the West in a fitful, luckless odyssey of short-lived jobs and failed businesses. The Power boys — Tom and older brother John — missed the three R's to hire out as cowboys, freighters, and blacksmiths.

Ending up in Arizona in the teens of the 20th century, young Tom farmed, competed in small-town rodeos, sold bootleg whiskey in Globe, ran a mine and stamp mill at Klondyke, and worked as a ranch hand at a dozen far-flung spreads. Of medium height, rawhide lean, gregarious, and handy as a shirt pocket, Tom was welcome wherever there was work. What he had missed in book learning, he made up for in an encyclopedic knowledge of the geography of central Arizona and the borderlands.

By 1918 the Powers reunited for one last toss of the dice. At a gold mine and grazing headquarters in Keilberg and Rattlesnake canyons high in Arizona's Galiuro Mountains, 55-year-old Jeff Power awaited delivery of a boiler for processing his high-grade ore. Death by now had taken two more women from Jeff, his mother (killed by a runaway horse) and daughter, Ola May (by food poisoning), but Jeff still had two strong sons, John, 27, and Tom, 25. Living and working with them was a discharged U.S. Army cavalry scout, Tom Sisson, age 54.

At the Power place, 25 primitive miles from the nearest tiny community, World War I seemed a world away. But from a secondhand newspaper the Power boys learned that they were required, along with all American men their ages, to register for the Selective Service draft. They attempted to comply with the law at Redington, but the postmaster (and official draft registrar) told them not to register, that they would be called if needed.

To the north, on the other side of the Galiuros, people saw it differently. While their own sons were registering for military service, the Power brothers were draft dodgers — in the slur of that day, "slackers."

Buoyed by inflamed local public opinion, Deputy U.S. Marshal Frank Haynes asked Graham County Sheriff Frank "Mack" McBride to help him arrest the Power boys. Ostensibly

JOHN POWER IN HAPPIER TIMES.

to assist in the investigation of Ola May Power's mysterious death, McBride brought along his regular Deputy Martin R. Kempton and volunteer Deputy T.K. Kane Wootan. The night of February 9, 1918, the posse climbed up and over a mile-high pass in the Galiuros and down into Rattlesnake and Keilberg canyons. In the predawn, in a light snowfall, the lawmen dismounted, tied their horses, and crept up to the corners of the Powers' two-room, chinked-log cabin whose canvas doors were faintly backlighted by the glow of a coal oil lamp.

What happened in the next few minutes has fueled controversy for eight decades. But most damning of the law operation was the later testimony of Marshal Haynes himself. He unintentionally described a police procedure seriously flawed by poor planning, questionable legality, and reckless execution. Haynes averred:

• The lawmen did not identify themselves as such, and gave no warning.

• Their approach frightened a young Power horse that was wearing a bell.

• Jeff Power, dressed in his long johns and cradling a carbine, stepped out of a doorway.

• "Throw up your hands!" shouted a lawman, and Jeff Power obeyed.

• Several gunshots rang out. Power collapsed. Then a firefight of 20 or 30 more shots ensued.

• Fearful of the ominous silence that abruptly fell over the scene, Haynes raced a horse to town to spread the alarm.

Tom Power's story, although from an entirely different point of view, was essentially the same. He said that inside the cabin everybody was abed but Jeff, who was lighting kindling in the fireplace and stove. Jeff heard the clanging bell on the running colt, assumed a cougar was on the prowl, grabbed his rifle, and dashed to the door. The cry, "Throw up your hands!" was immediately followed by a gunshot that felled Jeff Power. The brothers rolled out of their bunks and the battle was on. John went to help his fallen father and was driven back by a volley. One slug ripped off half the bridge of his nose and another splattered his face and left eye with wood splinters. Despite his wounds, he quickly sent two shots to each front corner of the cabin.

Of himself, Tom said he grabbed his rifle only seconds before a slug smashed through a windowpane and filled his left eye with glass shards. With his good eye he perceived a silhouette outside, let go one shot, and ducked.

Some moments later (according to Tom): "There was no sound from outside. We went to the door and peered out cautiously. It was eerily silent. We could see our father's body lying a few feet from the front of the cabin. We could also dimly see the outlines of two other bodies. Besides both of us having had our left eyes seriously injured, it was still not daylight." Sisson, Tom swore, never left his bunk to fight.

The Power boys first determined that their father was

TOM POWER AT WORK ON THE RANCH.

mortally wounded. Then in the gloom they identified the dead. "We couldn't believe it. One of them was T.K. Wootan. Another one was Sheriff Frank McBride, whom I had campaigned for. We did not know the third man [Deputy Kempton]." Tom said they were unaware that a fourth officer, Haynes, had been present and was galloping away.

If it was self-defense, why did the Powers and Sisson run? Tom maintained that the Powers had openly feuded for several years with Kane Wootan. Now they, Wootan's open enemies, and a couple of draft dodgers at that, had killed Wootan, plus the county sheriff and a deputy.

"Knowing what the general reaction would be . . . we decided to go to Tucson and turn ourselves in to Sheriff Rye Miles. We had known him for a long time and he was a good friend of our father's. We were sure we would get fair treatment from him."

History, goes an old saying, is written by the survivors. All that the greater world knew, or cared, was that duly authorized lawmen and upstanding civic leaders had gone to a hideout of defiant slackers, attempted to serve a warrant, and were slain. Sheriff McBride left a widow and seven children; Kempton a widow and seven; Wootan a widow and four. As the *Graham Guardian* reported, "Preparations were made at once to send out a posse to get the murderers, dead or alive."

Tom and John Power and sidekick Sisson took flight. They gathered up the slain posse's mounts and weapons, threw together trail packs, and descended the Galiuros southward, setting off a manhunt that would cover some of the Southwest's most rugged terrain.

After dark on February 10 at Redington (Tom claimed), they learned that a general alarm had been spread by telephone and that Sheriff Harry Wheeler of adjacent Cochise County had loudly vowed to run down and kill the fugitives.

"That is when," said Tom, "we decided to try for Old Mexico."

Little did they know that 3,000 men, in the greatest manhunt in Arizona's history, were mustering all around them. Tom Power's familiarity with the land came into play. The riders pushed south up the San Pedro Valley, slipped through the Little Dragoon Mountains, abandoned the mule, stole a rancher's horse, and crossed the Southern Pacific railroad tracks near Cochise.

Meanwhile, newspapers printed special editions with the latest sensations: companies of cavalry departing Fort Huachuca and other military posts, bloodhounds on the San Pedro trail, the killers' tracks found through cut barbed-wire fences, truckloads of fresh horses shipped where needed, roadblocks and canyon ambushes thrown across possible escape routes.

Incredibly (as reported by Tom): "At Chiricahua West Wall, we came upon a large posse. There were trucks, cars, and horses. The posse had built a fire, and had lighted lanterns. Three of them were wide-eyed, sleeping with their eyes open. They made no effort to pursue us."

In darkness, the fugitives reached the Chiricahuas, a

major north-south range lofting to 9,795 feet elevation. Surely they would be caught when "we saw a car loaded with men coming toward us. Guns were sticking out on each side of the car. The car was about 200 yards from us when it turned off on a road to the left."

Once in the Chiricahuas, Tom Power decided that their horse tracks would give them away. So the men fled on foot. Nearly every day and night brought a close call.

"One night we were bedded down in big round rocks in a creek bed," Tom recalled. "Before we could get away a large body of men and horses were walking over us. All we could do was lay there motionless and hope the horses were trained like good cow ponies — never to step on a man. We were so close we recognized some of the men in the posse, but they never saw us, and not one of their horses would put a hoof on us."

So it went for a week or more. Both Tom and John, especially John, were in constant agony with their eye injuries. Tom Sisson, fabled Indian scout, had little sense of direction. Tom had to lead, past patrols of soldiers, over the snow-covered summit, and out of the eastern foothills at a place called Portal. They bought food at some houses, pilfered it at others, and at least twice butchered beeves. At the crossroads named Rodeo, they entered New Mexico and swept in a looping arc across Hidalgo County, through the pass between Big Hatchet and Alamo Hueco mountains, and across the border into the state of Chihuahua, Mexico.

Their shoes fell apart and they wrapped their feet in canvas. They had but one canteen among them in a seemingly waterless high desert. John's wound filled his whole head with throbbing, unbearable pain. By the morning of March 18, they were 20 miles south of the border and actually heading back to the United States to surrender when by chance appeared a patrol of Troop I, 12th Cavalry, Lt. Wolcott P. Hayes commanding.

"The party was about 20 yards away," recounted Tom, "when we stood up and raised our hands. The sergeant was still afoot. Lieutenant Hayes literally fell off his horse, along with the rest of the soldiers who were mounted. Every one of them drew his .45 automatic pistol. They were so frightened their pistols were shaking in their hands. I told them to be careful with their guns, that someone could get hurt." In time, Troop I divided the $7,000 in rewards.

At Safford, the suspects were locked in cells and displayed to curious townspeople lined up for hundreds of yards. The wounded brothers did receive a measure of medical care, but they would not be allowed to bathe until they reached the state prison two months later.

Their conviction was never in doubt. They were allowed a lawyer and granted a change of venue to nearby Clifton in the next county. The Powers and Sisson were permitted to call but one minor witness, who was disqualified. Prosecution witnesses were so convincing, the jury deliberated just 30 minutes. Guilty, murder one. Arizona had recently outlawed capital punishment, so the most severe punishment available was life imprisonment. The trial transcript soon vanished, never to be seen again.

On May 21, 1918, Tom Sisson, prisoner number 5172, Tom Power, number 5173, and John Power, number 5174, were processed into the state prison at Florence, Arizona.

As an honorably discharged veteran, Sisson in time rated an Army pension, and he lived so long (to 87 years by the date of his death in prison, January 23, 1947), his estate had grown to $10,000, which he left to John Power. Sisson's prison behavior was unblemished.

So too was that of the Powers, except for a couple of brief escapes. Tom and John together ran off from a prison trusty gang and (briefly afloat on a rope-lashed raft) followed the Colorado River into Mexico. They got all the way to Mexico City, but were captured when they chanced a crossing into Texas.

In all, the brothers served more than 42 years of hard time, no reductions for invaluable prison labor and good behavior.

**THE POWER BROTHERS BACK ON THEIR RANCH
AFTER FINALLY BEING RELEASED FROM PRISON.**

Blinded in one eye (as was his brother), Tom spent his spare hours reading law and corresponding. His studies filled entire file cabinets with meticulously cross-referenced clippings, case citations, and arguments the defendants were never allowed to give at their trial. Ever the talkative one, Tom remained the optimist while his shorter, smaller, grumpier older brother grew inward. John became almost silent.

For an age that accepted as normal the release of convicted first-degree murderers after an average of seven years imprisonment, the elderly "Power boys" were allowed but one perfunctory parole hearing; their parole was summarily denied. A few sympathetic journalists wrote about their unusual incarceration. In 1960, the Powers got their second hearing, at which descendants and elder friends of the slain officers pleaded for forgiveness. The Power brothers, too, asked to be forgiven.

Limited freedom as parole did not come until April 27, 1960. Like Van Winkles wakened from a prolonged sleep, the brothers tried to meld into a culture of interstate highways, jet airplanes, universal television, rhinestone cowboys, and pen-fattened cattle. Well into their 70s, around their familiar old haunts in Arizona and New Mexico they tried to put their hands to what they knew: metalsmithing, horse training, cow punching. Arthritis, in time, crippled John and kept him home. John made peace with his lot — at least he was out of prison.

But Tom would not be satisfied with the relative freedom of parole. Its restrictions and implied guilt galled him. So he traveled and wrote and argued for nine long years, to whatever person he thought might effect a full pardon and restore all rights of citizenship.

At last in 1969, 51 years after the gunshots in the Galiuros, Governor Jack Williams pardoned the Powers. Said the governor to the press, "Who will ever know the right and the wrong of it?"

First thing, the brothers went to Graham County Courthouse and registered to vote.

John would live as an invalid until 1976. But that was not the style of Tom Power's departure.

On election day in September 1970, Tom traveled 120 round-trip miles by Jeep and car to cast his first-ever ballot. Three days later, he died of a heart attack.

Tom Power's days of running were done.

CHAPTER THIRTEEN

The Four-day Gun Battle at Ray, Arizona

*Pete Smith stole a horse and threatened
death to anyone who followed him,
setting off a running gun battle that left
seven men dead in the hills above the
small mining towns of Ray and Sonora.*

BY   LEO   W.   BANKS

⟫◦⟪

T HE MORNING OF AUGUST 19, 1914, PROMISED ANOTHER
hot day in Ray, Arizona, as Constable Phineas Brown
saddled his mount and rode into the Pinal Hills above
town. He was headed toward Pete Smith's camp in Devil's
Canyon to arrest Smith, a half-Mexican woodcutter who had
stolen a horse and galloped out of town threatening death to
anyone coming after him. Accompanying Brown was Will
Landry, a 17-year-old French boy who saw the theft take place
and could identify the black mare.

As the two rode into the canyon, they were met with a
warning that Smith and other woodcutters were drunk and
dangerous.

"I don't care," said Brown. "I'm not afraid."

Yet by noon that day, Brown and his young companion
were dead, shot down in a well-orchestrated ambush that set
off a firestorm of killing that wouldn't end until at least seven
men lay dead.

News of Brown's murder reached the copper-mining town
of Ray later that afternoon. A rancher named Lakel had heard
four shots fired in rapid succession and, after a pause, two more,

near Smith's camp. Lakel knew that Brown had gone into the camp to arrest Smith and that the shots signaled trouble. Then Lakel spotted two Mexicans riding down the canyon. One of them, Pete Smith, was on the constable's horse. Lakel hid in the brush.

After watching the Mexicans cross Mineral Creek, leave the horses on a mesa, and scamper into a gulch out of sight, Lakel hurried back to town.

The citizens of Ray, as well as those in the nearby communities of Hayden, Globe, Kearny, and Florence, were stunned at the news. Brown was a popular and respected lawman.

But was he really dead? Perhaps not. After all, Lakel never saw a body. Even as an angry citizens' posse gathered to track the bandits, Ray's faithful whispered prayers of hope that Brown was still breathing. But those hopes fell as quickly as Brown. The posse found his body at the mouth of the canyon, a bullet hole in his right lung.

They rode on into a narrow pass, where they were stopped by the pop-pop-pop of rifle fire that kicked up dust around their horses' hooves. No men were hit, but Deputy George O'Neill's horse was shot from under him. Curley Henderson, another member of the posse, located the sniper, traded rifle shots with him, and finally shot the bandit dead.

It was Smith, the horse thief. On his body, Henderson found Brown's Winchester and ammunition belt and, nearby, Brown's horse. The remaining members of the Mexican band jumped from their positions and fled over the perilous rocks deep into the canyon.

As grisly as the manhunt had already been, it soon worsened. The pursuing posse discovered the body of Will Landry. He had been stripped clean of his possessions, tied to a tree, and shot 17 times. One of the lawmen who found Landry later said: "The body and the tree trunk from which it had been suspended were riddled with bullets. The work was plainly that of the most cruel and depraved of murderers."

Then, to their shock and grief, the posse found two

more corpses, Earl Miller and Frank Bacon. Both worked as timekeepers at the Ray Consolidated Mine and lived in camps in Devil's Canyon.

According to news reports, their deaths were due to nothing more than ill fortune. As the (Globe) *Arizona Record* reported: "The fleeing Mexicans evidently mistook them for officers and shot them without parley."

The shootings spread over several days and pursuit of the bandits involved posses from three counties. Nightfall brought more anxiety as word raced through Ray that the Mexicans had been reinforced by a number of "idlers" and wood-haulers from neighboring mountains. How many gang members were there? No one knew for sure.

Other gossip had it that one of the Mexicans still on the run was headed for Florence and another was holed up in an impregnable position near Superior, surrounded by 60 officers.

Everyone feared that more blood would almost certainly be spilled dislodging him. Meanwhile, newspapers described a town heavy with tension.

"Business in Ray was at a standstill and the streets were absolutely deserted last night," reported *The Arizona Republican*. "Those men who were able to fight were summoned to the canyon, in a desperate effort to bring the slayers of Brown to justice.

"Those who were left were guards against a possible conflict with the inhabitants of the Mexican suburb of Sonora, across the river. Confusion and excitement reigned."

Rumors of race riots were rife. Relations between Anglo and Mexican workers in the mining camps near Ray had always been strained, if not openly hostile, and the electric atmosphere created by the shootings did nothing to calm them.

The tone was set by *The Arizona Republican*: "At midnight, when communication with Ray closed, every white man capable of carrying a rifle and riding a horse, was in Devil's Canyon, facing a force of armed Mexicans, entrenched about the camp of the woodcutters, who had started the trouble by stealing a horse." In another report, *The Republican* took leave of its editorial senses with inflammatory and ridiculous commentary on Landry's murder:

"This is described as characteristic of the actions of the depraved Mexican criminal. Most outlaws believe in dispatching their victims with one clean shot through a vital spot. Not so with the brother from across the border.

"His method is fiendish, cruel beyond words. He prefers to wound and torture and let death come rather from the accession of physical shocks and pain than by any sudden blow."

A news bulletin out of Hayden even reported that eight citizens of Ray lost their lives in rioting that erupted following the news of Brown's death and subsequent excitements.

But no riots took place. Ray resident F.E. Rich told *The Arizona Republican* that the Mexicans started shooting because they were drunk, and for that reason alone the trouble erupted:

"The American element is not stirred up over the killing," Rich said. "I heard no hostile sentiments expressed. Of course if there are any cracks made about Brown deserving what he got, there may be a few fist fights. But so far as I could see, everything was peaceable in Ray."

Meanwhile, in the Pinal Hills, lawmen closed in on the desperate bandits. Soon, a sixth man was dead. He was Ubaldo Amaya, Smith's half-brother, said to be an accomplice in the theft that started the bloody rampage. He refused to surrender to the pursuing posse and was shot.

The fugitive band again fled, this time splitting up to elude capture. The posse split in response. Believing the bandits would try to dodge into Sonora, a suburb of Ray populated by Mexican miners, O'Neill stationed some of his men in the hills above the town.

In the ensuing chase and still more gunplay, another Mexican was killed, although his name was never known. Subsequent press reports referred to him only as the unknown Mexican.

In all, it took four days to subdue the renegade band

and considerably longer to sort out the identities of all its members. Shortly after the shooting stopped, various theories surfaced to explain the killing spree. Pinal County Sheriff Henry Hall believed that Smith stole the horse and intentionally paraded it through Ray to make sure everyone noticed. Smith's intention was to get Brown to chase him into the hills, where a trap was set.

Hall said that Brown had intimate knowledge of a murder at the Carney Mine for which Smith was the chief suspect. Smith's half-brother, Ubaldo, was also believed involved in the Carney murder.

Another published theory was that the trouble began in the copper-mining town of Cananea, Mexico. Brown is said to have intervened in a dispute between the mining company and Mexican workers, resulting in the shooting deaths of 30 Mexicans. Pete Smith was rumored to have been in Cananea at the time of this trouble.

If the origin of the bad blood is in doubt, the result is not: at least seven dead, possibly eight. Reporters from several newspapers converged on the area, and in the atmosphere of confusion and near panic, their accounts often conflicted on the names of the dead, and even their numbers.

But the final chapter in the Ray tragedy wasn't played out until the following year. On December 10, 1915, Ramon Villalobos, convicted of the murder of Constable Phineas Brown, was hanged at the Arizona State Penitentiary at Florence, the first inmate put to death there.

Villalobos, wearing a bouquet of roses around his neck, proclaimed his innocence to the end. Before the trapdoor was sprung, he hugged his executioners and said, "I have killed no one. I forgive everybody."

The Riverside Stage Murder

CHAPTER FOURTEEN

The Riverside Stage Murder

Violent and inept stage robbers killed a shotgun guard, left part of the loot in the strongbox, and blazed an obvious getaway trail. And there was no chance of their escaping retribution when 100 of Florence's finest citizens showed up at the jail with a rope.

BY LEO W. BANKS

THE RIVERSIDE STAGE ROBBERS BOTCHED THEIR JOB FROM start to finish and left behind a trail of clues that a goldfish could have followed. But death, not blundering, was the chief legacy of this frontier stickup.

The robbers turned murderers when they gunned down a shotgun guard, then two of them became victims when a mob of Florence's finest citizens yanked them from their cells and lynched them. Within four months of the first bloodletting, six men were dead and two more wounded.

Friday, August 10, 1883. At 8:45 P.M., the Globe-bound stage pulled out of the Riverside station, 35 miles east of Florence. Nothing seemed amiss to driver Watson Humphrey and express messenger Johnny Collins, who was perched atop a Wells Fargo treasure box containing more than $3,000 in gold, silver, and currency.

Just after Humphrey lashed his team across the Gila River, a shotgun boomed. No warning. No words spoken. Collins took the charge in the chin and neck, and slumped dead over the wealth he was sworn to protect.

100

Humphrey jerked back on the reins as two men wearing gunny-sack masks sprang from the brush. One of them leveled a Winchester and began firing wildly at Humphrey. One bullet cut his whip stock in half and another grazed his thigh.

After seven rounds, Humphrey screamed, "For God's sake, stop shooting! You've killed one man, what more do you want!?"

From then on it was business.

Passenger Felix LeBlanc poked his head from the coach and received a command to step down or die. He emerged reaching for the stars.

"Boys, don't shoot," the frightened LeBlanc stuttered. "I will give up."

Next, the robbers ordered him to retrieve the express box. But with Collins' body lying atop it, LeBlanc was unable to hoist the box on his own. Humphrey moved to assist, asking to first lower Collins' body to the ground. The robbers refused, threatening to kill both men if they didn't get at the box, and fast.

When it was finally heaved over, the robbers handed LeBlanc a hatchet to break the lock. He took three licks, but the steel held. The robbers gave him powerful incentive to make the fourth blow count.

"You s.o.b.," one of them said, raising his firearm. "If you don't break it this time, I will bore you through." LeBlanc took a mighty swipe and the lock snapped off.

The *Arizona Weekly Enterprise* reported that the outlaws departed with $2,000 in silver and $500 in gold, but left $620 in currency in the box, one of several almost inexplicable errors.

The blundering bandits also showered the murder scene with evidence — including a pair of leather saddlebags and a belt full of Winchester cartridges — then virtually telegraphed their getaway route.

Hours after the robbery, residents of Dudleyville, 18 miles south of Riverside, reported seeing two men, with pistols drawn, gallop through town on lathered horses. Investigators also found a nickel-plated shotgun shell near the San Pedro Road.

Pinal County Sheriff A.J. Doran knew where to lead his

posse — L.G. Redfield's ranch in the high timber of the Galiuro Mountains, a rumored hideout for gunmen and road agents of all sorts. The lawmen arrived expecting a fight. But the men they encountered — Redfield and Joe Tuttle, an ex-stage driver from Florence — were, according to the *Enterprise*, "meek as doves and shook from head to foot" as they denied knowledge of the crime.

They were wasted words. Doran searched the property and found a U.S. Mail bag and a recently discharged shotgun stashed in a manure pile. The two were cuffed and taken to Florence, along with Frank Carpenter, Redfield's nephew.

The suspect list would eventually include two more men. The first was Red Jack Almer, also referred to as Elmer, a drinker and gambler who'd been hanging around Florence the week before the robbery.

In that time he managed to arouse the suspicion of every conscious individual he encountered. Using the alias Jack Averill, he made himself a fixture at the office of the stage line, watching Wells Fargo agents load the Globe coach.

The *Enterprise* reported that on the day of the robbery, when Red Jack saw that it required two men to lift the treasure box into the boot, "he suddenly concluded that he must be on that stage."

The robbers' plan was for Red Jack to board the stage only if the box was stuffed. His confederates, waiting at the big wash just short of Evans Station, would stop the coach if they saw Jack aboard wearing a red shirt with a white kerchief around his neck. And Jack was to burst into loud singing as the coach neared the wash.

The plan collapsed when the concealed gunmen were unable to hear Jack's operetta, and the coach rumbled on unmolested. After learning that Jack really was aboard, the two gunmen rode ahead and prepared to waylay the stage after the Riverside stop.

As for Almer, he made two mistakes guaranteed to put lawmen at his heels. When the coach stopped at Evans Station, he asked if two men had left a horse for him. When the answer was no, Jack flew into a rage, promising vengeance if they "failed to keep their agreement."

He left the station on foot and paid a boy he encountered $10 to take him to Redfield's ranch. Jack blabbed to the boy that he'd steal a horse if necessary, but he had to reach Redfield's that night.

The second suspect, Charley Hensley, was a hard case who often rode with Almer. He was the one who tried with such futility to kill Humphrey. The shotgun murderer was Tuttle, who collapsed under the questioning of Wells Fargo detectives and confessed. Redfield, Carpenter, and Almer were accessories.

Word of Johnny Collins' killing loosed dark winds in Florence. *Arizona Enterprise* editor Thomas F. Weedin, a friend of the murdered guard and a member of Doran's posse, did his best to darken them further.

His coverage of the events was lurid and inflammatory. "Guilt's Iron Fangs Engulf His Shrinking Soul," blared the headline above the account of Tuttle's confession. But Weedin went much further, declaring on the authority of no good man that justice through the courts was "uncertain," and that the public willed a hanging.

"As soon as it shall be positively known that the prisoners are the guilty ones," Weedin wrote, "they shall be taken out, given a fair trial before a citizens' committee, and promptly executed."

Weedin did everything short of hammer the gallows. But he couldn't have envisioned the bizarre manner in which the executions played out.

At 5 A.M. on September 3, Deputy U.S. Marshal J.W. Evans showed up at the Florence jail with a legal writ, signed by a Maricopa County judge, ordering the immediate release of L.G. Redfield.

Undersheriff G.L. Scanland, who'd been sound asleep, found himself confronted with a federal agent backed by seven armed riders. Among them was L.G. Redfield's brother, Hank,

NEWSPAPER EDITOR THOMAS F. WEEDIN HELPED
PURSUE THE KILLERS, WITH THE POSSE AND IN PRINT.

who'd somehow managed to convince Marshal Evans that unless he proceeded to Florence with a writ, Redfield would be unjustly hanged.

A befuddled Scanland delayed as long as he could, and a long confrontation brewed. At 9:30 A.M., after word had spread through town that Redfield was about to dance away, a hundred citizens shouldered firearms and marched to the jail.

Hank Redfield would have fought the hardest to spare his brother, but he'd dashed off to Picacho to telegraph for reinforcements. With him gone, the remaining possemen relented to the mob, which placed Scanland under arrest and surged into the cells.

Redfield eyed the vigilante executioners and said: "Well, boys, I guess my time has come."

Much more emotional, Tuttle dropped his face into his

hands and sobbed. "Let me talk!" he begged. "Give me time to talk!"

"You didn't give poor Collins time to talk," a voice shot back, "and we will serve you the same way."

The mob looped two ropes over a ceiling brace in the jail corridor, and there the prisoners strangled until they died. Carpenter, a young man barely out of his teens, was spared.

Outside, after the deed was done, a member of the mob walked up to Evans and taunted, "Redfield and Tuttle are in there. You can have both of them now."

Even though none of the citizen-killers wore masks, a coroner's jury ruled that Redfield and Tuttle came to their deaths at the hands of "unknown men."

But Red Jack and Hensley were still on the loose. Four weeks later, a miner named T.M. Jeffries spotted them in the Sulphur Springs Valley and wired Pima County Sheriff Bob Paul in Tucson.

With a hastily assembled posse, Paul hopped a train to Willcox and received another lead: The fugitives, in desperate need of provisions, planned to buy supplies from a freighter near Percy's ranch.

Paul and his men hid underneath the freight wagons, and at 9 P.M. on October 3, the robbers rode up. Paul hollered for them to surrender, but Red Jack and Hensley had vowed not to be taken alive and stuck to it.

"Trapped, by God!" Jack yelled, and began firing.

"The whole posse fired a volley in the dark and the men were heard to fall," Paul told the *Phoenix Weekly Herald*. "Red Jack fell within 20 feet of the wagon. Hensley fell 25 yards from the wagon. Then we kept shooting at their flashes. . . . I was satisfied that both were mortally wounded. Just then [Deputy] Laird got hit in the calf of the right leg. The bullet went right through the boot-leg and made a wound two inches long."

Red Jack was dead, but Hensley, bleeding heavily from a bullet wound in his groin, scrambled away. The next day, in a canyon eight miles from Percy's, he ambushed the pursuing posse with an opening shot that felled Paul's horse beneath him.

"The first I knew of his whereabouts was his shot," Paul said. "I could only see the smoke of his gun."

Hensley made a brave but foolish stand. He was lying on his belly in a gulch, shooting right up the hill toward the posse. He was wide open to their fire and got a bullet through the chest. One of the posse men ran to inspect the body and yelled back to Paul, "Don't shoot, he's deader 'n Hades!" Hensley had been hit by 11 bullets.

The chase was at last complete. Only one of the Riverside robbers remained alive. But Frank Carpenter's time was coming, too. In November, while in the Florence jail awaiting trial for aiding in the holdup, he died under circumstances that are still suspicious.

Some believe he was beaten and mistreated by his captors. But the official version, never publicly questioned by the best citizens of Florence, was more benign. It held that Carpenter's heart simply stopped beating due to nervous collapse.

CHAPTER FIFTEEN

Charles P. Stanton, Arizona's Conniving 'Irish Lord'

The eloquent Irishman Charles P. Stanton rose to riches in central Arizona's mining frontier, but whenever there was a murder in the area, Stanton was somehow associated. The law could never pin the crimes on Stanton, but in his curious and violent end, justice finally was served.

BY LEO W. BANKS

━━━━◈◈◈━━━━

C HARLES P. STANTON WAS EITHER A DIABOLICAL KILLER with the moral capacity of a rattlesnake or a sharp-eyed immigrant who understood that the Territory of Arizona in the late 1800s was wide open to a man wanting to get rich.

However, most chilling of all was the possibility that he was both.

The question remains in doubt to this day. But many still find it suspicious that Stanton's rise to power in the gold camps of central Arizona should coincide with a string of violent acts so numerous that the *Flagstaff Champion* called them "a foul blot on this country and territory."

The story begins in 1863 when a gold-hunting expedition led by pioneer Abraham Peeples and the renowned scout Paulino Weaver stumbled onto Antelope Mountain, 85 miles north of Phoenix.

On their first day of digging, the men collected $1,800 worth of nuggets simply by scratching at the gravelly earth with butcher knives.

The Peeples party had discovered what would become the richest deposit of placer gold in Arizona.

It wasn't long before Antelope Mountain was nicknamed Rich Hill, and the towns of Weaver and Antelope Station sprang up as men rushed in to find their fortunes.

One of them was Stanton, a well-spoken Irishman whose secretiveness about his past threw the miners of the district into a fit of rumormongering.

Some said he was a graduate of the University of Dublin who became fluent in French and Spanish during his travels around the world on a tramp steamer.

Others said he was an escaped convict, a diamond swindler, even a candidate for the priesthood who was expelled from the seminary for immorality or for rifling the silver coffers.

He was called a gentleman, a gangster, the richest man in Arizona.

The truth about Stanton was never clear. But two aspects of his character stand out.

The first was his imperious manner, a trait enhanced by a thick brogue. He was hated by the miners around Rich Hill, who mockingly called him the Irish Lord.

He also had a talent for finding trouble. No murder or robbery could occur in the Weaver mining district without Stanton being in the middle of it. And in just about every case he was the rumored suspect because he stood to gain financially from the crime. But producing proof was something else again. Stanton would invariably stand and proclaim his innocence in the most haughty and purple terms.

His high airs and troublesome ways were displayed in a letter to the (Prescott) *Arizona Miner* of June 20, 1879, in which he complained about his March 6 arrest on a charge of stealing a gold specimen:

"It is regretted that Prescott, the capital of the territory,

THE HOTEL STANTON, IN THE 1990S LOOKING
MUCH THE SAME AS IT DID WHEN CHARLES STANTON
WAS MURDERED THERE IN 1886.

should be the refuge of every precarious vagabond who can, with impunity, raid therefrom on any part of the county, and pounce with the savage ferocity of the hyena, upon any selected victim, who invariably is a respected citizen, who finds himself in the short space of 24 hours, emblazoned by those rapacious vampires as a notoriously bad man."

Stanton came to Arizona from Nevada and settled in Yavapai County in 1870. He worked as an assayer at the Vulture Mill near Wickenburg before acquiring — some say stealing — a half-interest in the Leviathan Mine located just two miles from Rich Hill. When the Vulture Mill closed, Stanton built a cabin on Antelope Creek and moved there to work the Leviathan. It was there, as Weaver and Antelope Station boomed, that Stanton began accumulating the wealth that would allow him to claim the role of successful businessman and community leader.

Newspapers of the day furthered that image by referring to him as a "man of determined courage" and "as good a single hand talker as can be found . . . who always makes sense." His ability with the language helped him convince authorities that Antelope Station needed its own post office and that none other than Charles P. Stanton should be postmaster. Shortly after his appointment to that position in March, 1875, Stanton arranged to reroute the stage line past his store, and he changed the name of Antelope Station to Stanton. At its peak, the town had a population of 3,500, and money from the mining and related businesses piled up. But so did the bodies and the unexplained crimes.

Stanton was said to have cleverly engineered a showdown between G.P. "Yaqui" Wilson and William Partridge, operators of rival stage stops and stores in Antelope Station. As the story goes, a few of Wilson's hogs got loose and destroyed some of Partridge's property. At Stanton's urging, Wilson returned to Partridge's house to reimburse him for the loss. At the same time that he counseled Wilson to appeasement, Stanton had sent an emissary to Partridge with the message that his rival was on his way to kill him. The *Arizona Miner* for August 10, 1877, reported that the two men argued outside the house before Partridge chased Wilson into some brush and shot him to death.

Stanton's role in the feud was never doubted by respected Peeples Valley rancher Charles B. Genung, who heard Partridge's version of the shooting as the killer made his way to Prescott to surrender. Partridge said that Stanton had been stirring bad blood between the men for some time and was on hand doing the same thing the day of the shooting.

His motive — taking over the businesses run by both men — was temporarily thwarted when John Timmerman, a business partner of Wilson's, arrived to reopen his store, and Partridge's property was taken over by a newcomer named Barney Martin.

But the crimes attributed to Stanton continued in the coming years. A merchant in Weaver was burned out and driven from his land. A rancher lost his cattle to a mysterious range fire. Stagecoaches between Phoenix and Wickenburg were held up twice. Stanton was brought in for questioning for both stage holdups, but lawmen in Yavapai and Maricopa counties could never make their suspicions stick.

The rumors said that part of his criminal genius was staying in the background while the dirty work was done by a band of Mexican outlaws under his control. The gang, headquartered in Weaver and led by Francisco Vega, twice torched Barney Martin's stage station and was probably in on John Timmerman's murder.

In his book *Tales of Arizona Territory*, author Charles Lauer writes that Timmerman was on his way to Wickenburg carrying $700 in gold when he was shot in the back from ambush and his body set ablaze. Those who loathed Stanton were not surprised when he produced a will naming himself the beneficiary of Timmerman's estate.

But none of the crimes attributed to Stanton were as horrible as the murders of Barney Martin, his wife, and two children. The family set out toward Phoenix by wagon on July 21, 1886. Martin, who had sold his land along the Hassayampa River and shuttered his store, had decided to quit bloody Stanton for good.

After two weeks, newspapers were openly suggesting that the missing Martin family had fallen victim to another foul crime. They were correct. The burned-out wagon was found in the desert midway between the Hassayampa and Agua Fria rivers with four human skulls in the back. The entire family had been murdered and their bodies burned. Reaction to the Martin massacre was fierce. But, as usual, few hard clues existed.

Genung turned up a witness who said that a group of Mexicans had stopped at her house around the time of the killings, leading to the arrest of two men. But without sufficient evidence to hold them, they were set free. An outraged Genung named Stanton as the murderous mastermind, and he was taken into custody and charged with being an accessory to murder.

Territorial newspapers jumped to Stanton's defense, calling him "one of the most prominent citizens of the county" and arguing that "not a whit of evidence of any kind" had been found to implicate him. That much was true, and amidst a mixture of cheers and outrage, Stanton was released.

But by now so many Arizonans were convinced of his guilt, and his complicity with Vega, that citizen mobs were willing to act on their own to prove it. Longtime Arizonan Tom Molloy, writing in 1921 about the aftermath of the Martin murders, said that a group of Phoenix men "took a Mexican from the region of Stanton or Weaver, and hung him by the neck to a tree for an extended period in a vain attempt to compel him to disclose something tending to incriminate Stanton, Vega, and the others." Molloy concluded that no one was ever "brought to justice for those diabolical crimes — that is, not in a court."

That sly reference was to the events of November 13, 1886. At a little after 6 P.M. that Saturday night, an employee of Stanton's named Kelly answered a knock at Stanton's front door and found three Mexican men. Stanton, seated at a table just inside the door, invited them to enter.

Newspaper accounts said the shooting started immediately, with Stanton taking three slugs in the chest "in a triangular shape."

"I'm killed! Blow out the light!" he yelled to Kelly before collapsing dead on the floor.

Using the darkness for cover, Kelly got hold of a rifle and killed one of the fleeing assailants with a bullet through the window.

As with every incident in which Stanton was involved, the truth was lost behind a cloud of whispers and mystery.

"Again, dame rumor was busy," wrote Molloy. "It was said that Stanton had received all of the boodle from the Martin murders, and that he had failed and refused to divide the spoils with the man who had actually and foully won them, and that in revenge Stanton's co-murderers had killed him."

But that wasn't the only motive put forth. The *Arizona Champion* wrote that the dead man, Cisto Lucero, had vowed to kill Stanton for insulting his sister and that Cisto's father had also made an attempt on Stanton's life four months earlier.

Curiously enough, that failed effort occurred at the same time of the Martin massacre and the *Champion* story came tantalizingly close to linking Stanton with the Vega gang: "For a long time he [Stanton] possessed a great influence over the Mexican population there, but of later years has been in trouble and has claimed that his life has been in constant jeopardy."

No tears were shed for the despised Charles P. Stanton. He was gone and that was good, because so few could any longer trust his declarations of innocence.

In the late 1950s, the *Saturday Evening Post* bought the town of Stanton and gave it away in a jingle contest. The buildings still stand, six miles east of present-day Congress off State Route 89. So does an old cemetery filled with unmarked graves of men who possibly were put there by the Irish Lord himself.

John Benjamin Townsend, Indian Hunter

In the violent clash between
territorial settlers and Indians in Arizona,
John Benjamin Townsend was
among the deadliest men of either race
and is remembered as either
a hero or a barbarian.

B Y   L E O   W .   B A N K S

———❖———

J OHN BENJAMIN TOWNSEND WAS A PIONEER, FAMILY MAN, rancher, and killer. His skill at the latter is the reason he is remembered today. In his six years in Arizona Territory, Townsend single-handedly killed an estimated 36 Apaches.

He hunted them like deer, and with an aggressiveness that puts a chill into the working heart. Whether he should be considered Arizona's Achilles, as the men of his day believed, or a barbarian, would make a fine parlor debate. But the truth is, he was probably both, depending on the day.

Assessing Townsend's life and motives is made difficult by the haziness of his early years. Few details are known of his upbringing, and there are some legends to sort through. The most persistent is that he was a Cherokee, a fiction spread by, among others, Army Capt. John Gregory Bourke, who served in the territory in the early 1870s.

"He certainly had all the looks — the snapping black eyes, the coal black, long, lank hair and the swarthy skin — of the

**JOHN BENJAMIN TOWNSEND POSED
FOR THIS CALM PORTRAIT CIRCA 1870.**

full blooded aborigine," wrote Bourke in his memoirs, "with all the cunning, shrewdness, contempt for privation and danger, and ability to read 'sign' that distinguish the red man."

It sounded good, but the claim was false. Townsend's ancestors actually came from England. His father and mother were born in Georgia and Tennessee, respectively, and the family moved to Round Top, Texas, in the 1830s. John Ben was born in that state on June 28, 1835. He fought for the Confederacy in the Civil War. After his discharge, he married 15-year-old Elizabeth R. Vickers, and in 1867 the couple came west in a covered wagon.

The Townsends settled in the fertile Agua Fria Valley, 40 miles from Prescott. It was a hard life in a lonesome place ruled by Apaches who raided and killed as a way of life. But Townsend was more than willing to match their brutality.

Rather than wait for the marauders to strike at his family and property, he hunted them first. At full moons he often rode alone into the hills above his home to pick up the trail of prowlers and ambush them. He carried a double-barreled, muzzle-loading shotgun for which he hammered out lead balls and cut them into slugs the size of grains of corn.

But the Apaches often reached the Townsend ranch, sometimes driving off his horses and swarming through his cornfield and garden, carrying blankets to haul away their booty.

"They came like droves of cattle," said Clara Vroom, Townsend's daughter, in a 1947 interview. "Once they set a barn on fire. Another time my father shot and killed two of the raiders before they could leave the field."

Next morning Townsend brought two of his children, Clara and Dee, out to see the bodies as a reminder to always be wary. One of the dead Apaches had a big ring in his nose.

Another story about Townsend — possibly more folklore — has him working for Gen. George Crook as a scout. In his book, *The White Conquest of Arizona*, Orick Jackson writes:

"As the column came into the zone where the Indians had been located he [Townsend] broke loose and went at it single-handed. Returning, he displayed 15 scalps, while the soldiers had not a single victim to their credit. This incensed General Crook and he immediately discharged Townsend."

Jackson offers no further details of the supposed fight, and Crook doesn't mention it in his biography. But Vroom said her father often scouted for the Army and that the soldiers were glad to have him along.

Townsend's most celebrated battle came in June, 1871, when Apaches raided the Bowers Ranch, 16 miles east of Prescott. Two herders had just finished watering the stock in the creek below the ranch when a large party of Indians opened fire on them.

Herder John Gantt was killed immediately. His partner's mule was shot from under him, but the man got to his feet and escaped. The Apaches made off with 137 cows, horses, and mules.

The next day a posse of armed citizens, including Townsend, joined with 30 soldiers from Camp Verde. The men tracked the

Apaches 25 miles up the East Fork of the Verde River, and descended on their rancheria on the afternoon of June 8.

The attack took the Indians by surprise. After the first deadly volleys of rifle fire, Townsend led a charge into the camp, hollering for the men to club the wounded to death. A total of 31 Indians were killed, 15 by Townsend himself. The posse crossed the divide between the East Verde River and Tonto Creek and attacked the Apaches again the next day. They killed 25 more and recovered virtually all of Bowers' stock.

The most haunting story to come out of the expedition surfaced 59 years later, in a letter to Ora Townsend French, another of the pioneer's daughters. It was from Ed Wright, a member of the posse then living in Texas. He described the aftermath of the fight:

"There were six or seven teepees and the babies, six or seven in their baskets, were leaning against a big rock. It was always rulable then to kill the babies to stop the warfare, and the saying was 'kill the nits to get rid of the lice.'

"We drew straws to see who would kill the babies and your father got the straw that was to kill the first baby, and he laughed and said that was easy. He pulled his gun and pointed it at the baby's face. I was watching him and saw a peculiar look come over his face, and knowing him so well, I saw there was something wrong.

"He put his pistol back in his holster and said, 'You can call it heart failure or what you please, but if you want to kill those babies you can do it yourself.' The baby had smiled in his face. It wasn't heart failure, but he said 'when that baby smiled, my little girl, Ora, at home got between me and that baby.' He turned away and released all the rest."

Wright added that he, Townsend, and a third man roped the baby baskets above ground between two trees, away from wild animals, and some time that night the Apaches returned and got them. "You saved six or seven Indian babies," Wright wrote to Ora. "You were the heroine of baby canyon."

Townsend fell into a black mood after the fight. It didn't lift until he returned to his ranch.

Wright described the scene in his letter: "We got home about the middle of the afternoon, your father jumped off old Jerry, a big stallion, and ran in the house and came back on the porch with you in his arms and appeared to be relieved of his troubles."

Prescott was ecstatic at the number of Apache deaths. The *Weekly Arizona Miner* called it a "terrible but glorious slaughter." On Sunday, June 18, the town hosted a party for the citizen-militia that was later dubbed the Prescott Jubilee. The raucous celebration included rifles fired in proud salute.

Four days later, Townsend was given a brand new Henry rifle and 1,000 rounds of ammunition in appreciation. The stock bore a silver plate with the inscription: "Presented to J.B. Townsend by the citizens of Prescott, June 1871. Honor to the Brave."

Other territorial newspapers wrote of the expedition, some with a mixture of defensiveness and sarcasm. The (Tucson) *Arizona Citizen* for July 8, 1871, commented:

"The Camp Grant Massacre now has a sequel. What blood-thirsty wretches these Arizonans are? Isn't it shocking? And then to hold a meeting of public feasting and Thanksgiving over the slaughter of the Apaches! Oh, dear! And on the Sabbath, too! What will Vincent Colyer and Horace Greeley say? Nobody between the Colorado and the Rio Grande cares what they say. We are the people — and are satisfied for this time."

Little is known of Townsend's life after the fight. But Ed Wright did recount two illuminating incidents in his letter. One occurred in the mountains south of Ash Creek, when the two men ran into some antelope. Townsend shot one of them and yanked the animal's head up by its horns to inspect it. But it was only stunned.

"The buck jumped up and tried to butt him and slung him around in some cat-claw bushes," Wright wrote. "He hollered for me to shoot him."

VIOLA (MRS. JOHN) SLAUGHTER WITH THEIR ADOPTED INDIAN DAUGHTER, APACHE MAY SLAUGHTER. IT WAS AN APACHE CHILD LIKE THIS THAT STAYED TOWNSEND'S KILLING BRIEFLY.

But the two were in so desperate a fight that Wright couldn't get off a good shot. Finally he pressed his gun against the animal's shoulder and fired, killing it.

Townsend, badly cut up in the brawl, said to Wright, "Ed, I thought you was quick on the trigger, but I believe you are the slowest man I ever saw." He also remarked that he'd rather fight a half dozen Indians than one antelope buck in the cat-claw.

The second incident took place late in the fall of 1871. Wright, Townsend, and rancher Theodore Boggs went to Camp Verde for the sale of government horses. They passed a group of Indians at the edge of camp.

"As we rode by they were pointing toward your father," wrote Wright in his letter to Ora, "and Boggs said, 'John, they're talking about you,' and your father said, 'Yes, they know me.' I told him they would get him. He said, 'If you and Theodore are here when they get me, I want you to look after Lizzie and the children till they are provided for.' "

Townsend's words were prophetic. His end came September 16, 1873, one day after he left his ranch to hunt deer in the Bradshaw Mountains. He told Elizabeth he'd be back before dark. Several days later, his horse galloped back to the ranch, riderless. A search party found Townsend's decomposing body at Dripping Springs, west of Cordes and below Big Bug Creek.

The *Miner* of September 27 theorized that Townsend was on foot when he spotted some Apaches. He jumped on his horse and charged them, and a rifle bullet took him out of the saddle.

The paper noted that the ground around the body had been torn up by his horse's hooves, indicating that the "faithful animal stayed by his master until instinct and the smell of him made him understand that he for whom he had such love would never again ride him to victory over Apaches or to a successful hunt for game."

Townsend was 38, the father of five. His body was taken to Prescott for burial in the Masonic cemetery. The funeral cortege was followed by the 23rd Infantry band, 40 fellow Masons, and some 300 civilian and military personnel.

The send-off befitted a man who knew how to kill. It was a skill revered by everyone on the frontier, including Apaches. They thought so highly of Townsend as an enemy that they neither stripped nor mutilated his body, as was their custom.

But they did make off with his prized Henry rifle. It remains unrecovered to this day.

CHAPTER SEVENTEEN

Bob Leatherwood, the Little Giant

Small in stature and big in courage,
Bob Leatherwood pursued bad men,
Geronimo's renegade Apaches, and politics
with great fervor. Ironically, a runaway horse
carried him to his greatest fame.

BY LEO W. BANKS

⟫⟪

ROBERT N. LEATHERWOOD HARDLY CUT AN IMPRESSIVE figure. He stood 5 feet 5 inches and weighed 130 pounds. Even his Confederate uniform, which he proudly wore at important civic functions, accentuated his diminutive stature.

He had a sunken face, and his voice was so high-pitched it could shatter grandma's tea set. He looked more like a clerk at a dry-goods store than a pioneer legend.

But it was said of Leatherwood that he could lick his weight in wildcats. He was a lawman feared by outlaws from El Paso to the West Coast and an Apache fighter who led a band of volunteers in pursuit of Geronimo.

Leatherwood's most famous chase started on May 22, 1886, when a band of about 14 Apaches led by Geronimo raided the Rincon Mountain ranch of Juan Tellez, carrying off a nine-year-old boy.

Leatherwood and two other men led one of the first posses to ride out of Tucson after the Apaches. The band was composed of volunteers called the Tucson Rangers. *The Arizona Daily Citizen* described them as "determined avengers."

They whipped their horses to a full gallop and reached the Tellez ranch, located 15 miles southeast of Tucson, in less than two hours. Time was of the essence. If the Apaches were able to get far enough ahead, the kidnapped boy might never be recovered.

Years later, Octaviano Gastelum described what it was like to be held captive. After chasing his mother and stoning her until she fell unconscious into the canyon, the Apaches taunted Octaviano, saying, "Your mother is a good runner."

Then he watched as the Apaches took a cow, cut a nerve in its leg so that it could not stand, and began to skin it from both sides.

"When the blood ran, they got down and drank it like dogs. . . . Every once in a while they would punch me in the ribs to make me cry. . . . Geronimo whipped me as if I were a burro."

But the Tucson Rangers were close behind. Not far from the Tellez ranch, the posse burst onto the raiding party eating supper in a canyon. Shooting started. Octaviano felt a bullet whip past his ear. "The bullets were like firecrackers," he recalled.

The Rangers all jerked back on their reins, except for Leatherwood. He charged straight ahead into the Apache camp and sent the startled braves running. Cosulich wrote that Octaviano ran to the Rangers as the Indians fled up the mountainside.

The *Citizen* reported that three Apaches used rifles to hold off the Rangers' pursuit, with two of the Indians eventually mounting horses "and the third hostile hanging fast to the tail of one of the horses to assist his flight."

For several weeks, Leatherwood allowed Tucson to believe he'd committed an act of valor. He was feted as a hero. But he wasn't one for pretense, and Leatherwood eventually admitted that he'd actually lost control of his horse, meaning his stirring charge was entirely involuntary.

The Rangers spent much of the summer of 1886 chasing Geronimo through southern Arizona and into Mexico.

ROBERT N. LEATHERWOOD'S FLAWS
WERE SOMETIMES LUDICROUS, BUT THE
LITTLE MAN COMMANDED RESPECT.

Leatherwood himself led a party south of the border, but the Apache chief proved too wily, and the hunt ended in frustration.

When Geronimo surrendered to Gen. Nelson A. Miles early in September, the group returned to Tucson and disbanded.

"The boys have done some good work," reported *The Arizona Daily Star*, "and Lieutenant Leatherwood is entitled to great credit."

The Little Giant, as Leatherwood was called, was born in Clay County, North Carolina, on June 1, 1844. He spent his boyhood on a plantation, and during the Civil War served with the South's 37th North Carolina Infantry, perhaps as a scout.

At war's end, he roamed through Idaho, Wyoming, Colorado, New Mexico, and parts of Canada, briefly engaging in mining in Montana before landing in Tucson in May of 1869.

He bought a plot of land inside the walled pueblo and opened Leatherwood Stables, an enterprise that writer Bernice

Cosulich in her book, *Tucson*, said became known throughout the Southwest. The property was later the site of the Pima County Courthouse.

The nickname Little Giant derived from what Cosulich called Leatherwood's "fearless handling of lawbreakers."

In one case, he tracked two murderers for months, finally, according to contemporary M.M. Rice, "running them to earth in Death Valley, and single-handed, returning them in irons to the Tucson jail."

Doing good work was the story of Leatherwood's life, from his first political job to his final campaign in 1914, an unsuccessful bid for the Democratic nomination as state senator.

And his most lasting reputation was made in public affairs. He served in one office or another for more than a quarter-century, beginning with his election to the Village Council of Tucson in 1874.

He also won election as treasurer in 1878, served two terms as county sheriff and three in the Territorial Legislature. He was Tucson's mayor in 1880 when the Southern Pacific Railroad rumbled into town for the first time.

The hoopla that accompanied the first train — which arrived at 11 A.M. March 20, 1880 — was unprecedented. The 6th Cavalry band was on hand from Fort Lowell, cannons roared in greeting, and citizens shouted with glee as dignitaries gave speeches and raised glasses in toasts.

But it was Leatherwood's day. He'd worked hard to bring this modern wonder to the village, and was so frantic with excitement that he wanted to tell the world.

He sent telegrams to dignitaries throughout the United States, including President Rutherford B. Hayes, and around the world. One even went to the pope. It read:

"The Mayor of Tucson begs the honor of reminding your Holiness that this ancient and honorable pueblo was founded by the Spaniards more than three centuries ago and to inform your Holiness that a railroad from San Francisco, California, now connects us with the Christian world."

Amused by Leatherwood's boundless enthusiasm, a group of wags at Tucson's Palace Saloon drafted a fake reply:

"His Holiness the Pope acknowledges with appreciation receipt of your telegram informing him that the ancient city of Tucson at last has been connected with the outside world and sends his benediction, but for his own satisfaction would ask, 'Where the hell is Tucson?'"

For several days, Leatherwood couldn't bring himself to believe the reply was a hoax.

The Little Giant's political style fit his character: short, colorful, and effective. Tucson pioneer Mose Drachman recalled that Leatherwood usually campaigned on horseback or in an old buckboard.

"His regular companion on these stump-speech trips to the ranches about the country was a jug of good drinking whiskey," Drachman said, "which in those days, when throats of the outlanders were continually dust-coated, was a most convincing argument."

In remembrances published in *The Arizona Daily Star* in September, 1925, Drachman said that old-timers enjoyed watching the "doughty little bachelor" campaign for sheriff by sitting down with voters, chewing the end of his cigar, and nodding emphatically as he laid plans for the apprehension of evildoers.

Leatherwood once made a barnstorming trip to the mining camp of Quijotoa on what is now the Papago Indian Reservation. Cosulich says he walked into a crowded saloon, stacked a small table on top of a larger one, and a chair on top of both. Then he climbed up.

"Ladies and gentlemen," he called as every eye moved to the little man standing on the chair. "Well, I'm here. I came from Tucson. I'm going to stay until I go. I'm running for sheriff. Gentlemen, name your poison."

He tossed four $20 gold pieces on the bar and climbed down. He got the votes. Cosulich called it perhaps the shortest political speech on record.

Leatherwood knew his way around a saloon, and more importantly, he knew the hearts of the men he met there. One old acquaintance described him as a sage, with a droll, Will Rogers quality in his manner of expression.

At the same time, he was nearly illiterate. He once sent a letter to Maricopa County's sheriff, who couldn't read it and sent it back. Leatherwood, not recognizing his own handwriting, railed about the horrible penmanship.

"That damned man ought to write better," he groused. "I can't read this." That was mild for Leatherwood, who could cuss the skin off a black bear and back on again.

Another time he was drinking and playing poker in a saloon when the discussion turned to religion. An argument grew.

"I bet you $20 you can't recite the Lord's Prayer," Leatherwood said, and slapped his money on the table.

His oratorical opponent began, "Now I lay me down to sleep, I pray the Lord my soul to keep."

Leatherwood interrupted, "You win! You win!" He shoved the $20 across the table to great laughter around the room.

It would be hard to identify an issue in which Leatherwood did not play a role. He oversaw Arizona's exhibit at the St. Louis World's Fair in 1904, developed and promoted Tucson's gravity water system, and even established the town's first speed limit.

"Five miles an hour on horseback was deemed to be a fast enough pace for anyone," the *Arizoniana* magazine wrote in 1960.

As a member of the 13th Legislature, known as the "thieving thirteenth" for its use of bribery and favoritism, he helped defeat a scheme that would have blocked establishment of the University of Arizona in Tucson. Keeping the school might have constituted his greatest and most lasting political achievement.

When his public days ended, Leatherwood moved to Apache Camp near Mount Lemmon in the Santa Catalina Mountains north of Tucson. *Arizoniana* reported that after selling his mining claims there to the Copper Queen Mining Company, he stayed on as caretaker for the company.

His home was a cabin built from boards hauled from a nearby sawmill. When it fell apart, he moved into a tent house pitched in the middle of his peach orchard. He grew potatoes, rode his white horse, Pigeon, into Oracle, pored over newspaper accounts of American troops fighting in France, and bought liberty bonds.

Old friend Allan Jaynes once described Leatherwood as an "intense patriot" whose greatest regret was that he couldn't fight for his country in World War I.

On April 3, 1920, he traveled to Tucson, in keeping with his custom of celebrating Easter in town. That night he was in Rossi's restaurant when he complained of not feeling well.

A moment later his heart stopped beating. He was 75, the last of a frontier breed. Leatherwood was buried in his Confederate grays.

"His fame and that of the other pioneers of his type will be preserved forever in the annals of the romantic early history of Arizona," stated one newspaper tribute. "Those were days of real men and Bob Leatherwood was one of them."

CHAPTER EIGHTEEN

King S. Woolsey, Arizona's Fiercest Indian Fighter

Pioneer freighter, rancher, road builder,
and developer, King S. Woolsey believed
in protecting himself and his property
from Apaches and whoever else threatened him.
Honest in business and treacherous in battle,
Woolsey's methods of dispatching his enemies
were ruthless and unforgettable.

BY LEO W. BANKS

ING S. WOOLSEY WAS A TRUE PIONEER, ONE OF A HAND-
ful who shaped early Arizona. He lived up to his name.
He was a man of power who acted with the certainty
of a thunderclap.

Every account of the settling of the territory bears prominent mention of his name. He built public roads through unimaginable wilderness and carved ranches and farms from seemingly
hopeless desert.

He was among the first explorers of central and northern Arizona, made a fortune furnishing army posts with
supplies, lost a good portion of it in failed mines, but made
another fortune in flour and grist mills, and in real estate.

Between business ventures, he won election to the first
Territorial Legislature and was returned to the post four times,
earning a reputation for honest dealing.

At his death, *The Phoenix Herald* wrote that "a greater

calamity could not have befallen this community, than the death of this gentleman . . . who was associated with every enterprise that was for the public good."

But King Woolsey was both great and terrible. Like many pioneers, he was unencumbered by doubt or the niceties of law. He lived in a wild land and believed that his role was to tame it. If that meant taking lives, he took them.

Nowhere was this harsh ethic more evident than in his treatment of marauding Apaches. As a lieutenant colonel in the Territorial Militia from 1866 to 1869, his answer to their actions was uncomplicated: They should be exterminated, and he set about doing so with a brutality that earned him the title of Arizona's fiercest Indian fighter.

Details of the Alabama-born Woolsey's early days are sketchy and packed with legends. One such tale involves his parents deciding that their son should become a priest and packing the youngster off to a Catholic seminary. Woolsey was decidedly unimpressed and soon escaped to begin a life of adventure.

Another story has Woolsey joining an ill-fated force headed to Cuba with the intention of liberating the island from Spanish control. The teenager was captured and spent months in a Havana prison. He was released and put on a ship to California, where he worked as a miner.

Word of the discovery of mineral riches along the Colorado River brought him to Yuma in 1861. Woolsey's only possessions were his horse, a rifle, sidearms, and $5 in cash.

But before long the King was in business. He purchased a mule team and wagon, and won lucrative government contracts to deliver hay, beef, and mesquite beans to Fort Yuma.

Biographer John S. Goff notes that Woolsey was an ardent Confederate, but his sympathies were apparently not strong enough to overcome his desire to make money. He made an estimated fortune of $60,000 bringing supplies to Yankee troops.

**KING S. WOOLSEY LIVED VIOLENTLY
AND DIED OF A HEART ATTACK AT AGE 47.**

It seems the King had a knack for knowing where the money was. According to one story, he advised Henry Wickenburg where to hunt for gold. The result was the discovery of the Vulture Mine, the largest gold strike in Arizona history.

With his new wealth, Woolsey and a druggist named George Martin put down $1,800 in gold and bought the Agua Caliente Ranch, located on the Gila River 80 miles northeast of Fort Yuma.

There, Woolsey operated Arizona's first flour mill and brought the first threshing machine into the territory. The ranch became famous for its bubbling hot springs, described by Irish writer J. Ross Browne as "equal to the baths of Damascus or any other in the world."

Bob Cunningham, writing in *The Journal of Arizona History*, reports that Woolsey eventually opened a store across the river from the ranch at the old Stanwix Stage Station, which became the only civilian telegraph point between Maricopa Wells and Yuma. He also won contracts to build public roads, one of which ran all the way from Phoenix to Yuma, via Stanwix.

In 1863, with his fortunes high, Woolsey established the first ranch in northern Arizona, 15 miles east of Prescott, at Agua Fria. It earned him the distinction of Yavapai County's original settler.

He built Agua Fria like a fort as protection against mounting Indian hostility. Even so, the ranch was the scene of numerous raids in which Woolsey's stock was stolen or slaughtered.

Fighting was inevitable. As Goff noted, both of Woolsey's ranches were "located along well-established Apache plunder trails," and he possessed two traits common among pioneers: a strong belief in property rights and a "distinct inclination toward self-preservation."

Woolsey's first battle came as he and two other men were hauling a load of hay near an old overland mail stop on the Gila Trail called Burke's Station.

When the Apaches burst from ambush, Woolsey yelled, "Hold the mules, boys, and give me the gun!" King leveled a double-barreled shotgun and let loose with an errant blast. In his book *Adventures in the Apache Country*, Browne described what happened next:

"The leader of the Apaches, a warrior of gigantic stature and hideous features, rushed forward brandishing his war-club, and called upon his men to follow. Woolsey waited until the chief had approached within twenty paces, when he discharged the other barrel of his gun. Down tumbled the yelling savage, with a hole in his head."

Never one for subtlety, Woolsey tied a rope around the chief's neck and strung the body up to a mesquite tree. That incident — and an 1864 fight at Bloody Tanks, near today's Miami, in which Woolsey tricked his Apache adversaries into a parley, then signaled for his men to fire — solidified his reputation as a merciless enemy.

The Bloody Tanks massacre stemmed from Tonto Apaches stealing livestock from settlers in Peeples Valley and the area west of Prescott in the winter of 1863 and '64. Woolsey, at the head of a group of 30 Americans and 14 Maricopa, Pima, and Yuma Indians, chased the Apaches more than 100 miles over rough country into the Tonto Basin. Accounts of the incident vary widely, but the most often told story tells of Woolsey's group being surrounded by the Apaches at a small valley near present-day Miami. Woolsey sent a Yuma Indian named Jack to persuade the Apache leaders to come down to parley, telling them that the Americans had come to make peace and give gifts to the Apaches.

Woolsey and three of his men armed with concealed pistols left the others of his party about 200 feet behind with instructions to open fire when he gave the signal — raising his hand to his hat. As they were seated with about 30 Apache head men, an Apache came into the semicircle with two lances. Another Apache secretly distributed knives to the seated Indians. Then an Apache boy ran in with the message that the leader had ordered them all to leave the council because he wanted to kill all the white men and their allies.

Woolsey quickly gave the signal for the attack, and simultaneously shot the Apaches near him. The other three militia soldiers at the council followed suit, while their allies to the rear fired upon the Apaches in the surrounding hills. The number of Apaches killed was never tallied, but only one American died in the massacre.

Over the next five years, Woolsey organized and led several parties of settlers whose mission was simply to kill Apaches. Newspapers kept the citizens updated on each of the King's skirmishes, usually with a body count.

In one case, *The Weekly Arizona Miner* announced that Woolsey was leading a hundred men on a mission "to prospect for gold, silver, and copper-colored wretches."

The paper continued: "Here is the chance for loose-footed

gentlemen to explore the 'Heart of Arizona,' and maybe, thin the thick crop of Apaches."

Woolsey's exploits made good copy, particularly the story of John Donohugh, who was on guard duty at King's camp when he was stuck through the neck with an Apache arrow. The *Miner* wrote that Woolsey and several other men "rushed to the spot, guns in hand, and poured a volley into the rascals" to chase them off.

In another case, the *Miner* printed a thrilling account written by Henry Clifton, one of Woolsey's men.

"The boys of Company B . . . charged upon the redskins, first firing their rifles, and then rushing on them, pistols in hand," wrote Clifton. "The Indians made a faint show of resistance, and soon took to their heels, running up the canyon, where Company C was stationed, and were duly received by them, an Indian falling at nearly every shot, though he would usually get up and scamper off. The vagabonds can carry off an immense quantity of lead."

Some of Woolsey's actions, particularly his trickery, drew outraged criticism. Historian James Barney, writing in 1947, described the complainers as "Eastern religionists" who even made wild allegations that Woolsey had poisoned Apaches with strychnine.

Woolsey himself did little to conceal his purpose. "I fight on the broad platform of extermination," he said in an 1864 letter.

But Goff said this hatred extended only to Apaches, noting that one of Woolsey's best friends was the war leader of the Maricopa tribe, and his first wife was a Yaqui girl. Woolsey found 10-year-old Lucia in a canyon following her escape from a band of Apaches and took her to Agua Fria. She became his housekeeper and eventually his common-law wife, a relationship that lasted four years and produced three children.

Although it was illegal for a white man to marry an Indian, Woolsey's union with Lucia did little to tarnish his reputation.

His warlike ways, particularly his marksmanship, had made him a figure of heroism.

In 1893, almost 15 years after his death, the *Tempe News* called Woolsey "the finest rifle shot that ever walked the soil of the west," then described how he once shot a thread at 50 paces, dropping a swinging bullet tied on its end into a bottle.

The story of how Woolsey met his second wife, Mary Taylor, seems to come from the same storybook. It was August, 1869, and she was part of a wagon train bound for California with a man she'd agreed to marry.

But the trip had convinced Mary that marriage was a terrible idea, and she wanted out. A big man sitting up on his horse at the campfire heard Mary complaining and made her a proposition.

"Lady, if you want to leave these people, I'd take you," said King Woolsey. "I live a few miles west and will protect you."

She jumped onto the back of his horse, grabbed his belt, and rode off with him. Thereafter newspapers reported that Woolsey had traded "six sacks of flour or corn meal" for his bride. Mary subsequently "throttled that cohabitation" between Woolsey and Lucia.

Even after participating in the Apache wars, King Woolsey took part in several gruesome incidents that added to his repute.

In August, 1872, a man who had once worked at Agua Fria murdered a Mexican boy that Woolsey had raised. On the same day the boy was buried, Woolsey ordered the killer to dig his own grave and stand beside it.

Then, according to J.H. McClintock's 1916 history of Arizona, four of Woolsey's Mexican workers, armed with rifles, heard King's command and shot the man into his grave.

He executed his own justice again two years later when a stable man named Ventura Nuñez murdered the manager of Burke's Station. Woolsey tracked the killer for 60 miles and brought him back to Burke's, where he was identified as the killer, taken to a roadside mesquite tree, and strung up.

"The body hung for months," wrote McClintock. "The skeleton at last dropped from the rope and was buried by Mexican freighters, who placed a rough cross above the grave."

Woolsey ran for Congress in 1878, and newspapers again put heavy emphasis on his romantic pioneer past. The *Miner* wrote that he "came like so many other honest men, swinging a blacksnake over mules."

Woolsey finished fourth in the balloting. But the outcome, which he anticipated, didn't bend his spirit. He told *The Arizona Citizen* that on the day after the election he planned to "start 16 plows preparing the soil for a 2,000-acre wheat patch."

Woolsey only lived another year. When he died of a heart attack at age 47, he was one of the largest landowners in Maricopa County and considered one of the founders of Phoenix. But he's best remembered as an Indian fighter, efficient, savage, and smart, a man who saw a need to tame the territory and did so, no matter the cost.

INTRODUCTION

PAGE 7   Navajo County posse. Arizona Department of Library, Archives and Public Records, Archives Division, Phoenix, #98-0450D.

CHAPTER 1

PAGE 9   Murder scene. Arizona Department of Library, Archives and Public Records, Archives Division, Phoenix, #98-1677D.

PAGE 11   Town of Globe. Arizona Historical Society/Tucson, #61104.

CHAPTER 4

PAGE 27   Navajo family. Arizona Historical Foundation, University Libraries, Arizona State University, #G-779 N-4845.

CHAPTER 5

PAGE 33   Augustine Chacón. Department of Southwest Studies, Maricopa Community Colleges.

PAGE 35   Judge Owen T. Rouse. Arizona Historical Foundation, University Libraries, Arizona State University, #N-1370.

CHAPTER 6

PAGE 39   Gillette stage. Arizona Historical Foundation, University Libraries, Arizona State University, #LO-68.

PAGE 42   Francisco Renteria. Arizona Historical Foundation, University Libraries, Arizona State University, #G-863.

PAGE 43   Hilario Hidalgo. Arizona Historical Foundation, University Libraries, Arizona State University, #G-864 N-3052.

PAGE 45   Renteria and Hidalgo execution. Arizona Historical Foundation, University Libraries, Arizona State University, #G-865.

CHAPTER 8

PAGE 53   William S. Oury. Arizona Historical Foundation, University Libraries, Arizona State University, #THEO-47 N-2564.

PAGE 55   John Spring. Arizona Historical Society/Tucson, #28412.

PAGE 56   William Zeckendorf and family. Arizona Historical Foundation, University Libraries, Arizona State University, #B-238 N-2011.

CHAPTER 9

PAGE 63   Gravestone at Tombstone's Boot Hill. Arizona Department of Library, Archives and Public Records, Archives Division, Phoenix, #98-4017D.

CHAPTER 10

PAGE 73   Fleming "Jim" Parker's execution. Arizona Historical Foundation, University Libraries, Arizona State University, #G256.

CHAPTER 11

PAGE 76   Wham Robbery scene. Arizona Historical Foundation, University Libraries, Arizona State University, #BR-122.

PAGE 78   The Wham Robbery defendants. Arizona Historical Foundation, University Libraries, Arizona State University, #BR-39 BRN-91.

PAGE 80   William Breakenridge. Arizona Department of Library, Archive and Public Records, Archives Division, Phoenix, #96-3274D.

PAGE 81   William H. Barnes. Arizona Historical Foundation, University Libraries, Arizona State University, #G-329.

PAGE 82   Richard E. Sloan. Arizona Historical Foundation, University Libraries, Arizona State University, #B-141 N-948.

**LAWMEN AT THE HILLSIDE ENTRANCE
TO THE FIRST JAIL IN MIAMI, ARIZONA.**

VOLUME I

WILD WEST
COLLECTION

DAYS OF DESTINY
Fate Beckons Desperados & Lawmen

Many a newcomer journeyed West intent on molding his own future — grabbing life with both hands and producing opportunity. Shifty or bold, desperate or noble, given a trusty horse, a gun, and occasional friends, any man might stand a chance.

But every chain of events has one single day, perhaps a fleeting moment, when fate first points a decisive finger and the course of history changes. Delve into this collection of 20 Wild West tales and see how real-life desperados and lawmen faced momentous days that changed their lives forever.

Does the outlaw finally dance to his doom? Will the lynch mob hang the gambler who just killed a man? Does the kidnapped boy stay with the Apaches who stole him? Will the young mother become a stagecoach robber? Look back through time to see if you can spot when destiny dealt the final hand.

Softcover. 144 pages. Black and white illustrations and historical photographs. **#ADAP6 $7.95**

ARIZONA
HIGHWAYS
BOOKS

To order these books or to request a catalog, contact:
Arizona Highways, 2039 West Lewis Avenue, Phoenix, AZ 85009-2893.
Or send a fax to 602-254-4505. Or call toll-free nationwide 1-800-543-5432.
(In the Phoenix area or outside the U.S., call 602-258-1000.)
Visit us at www.arizonahighways.com to order online.

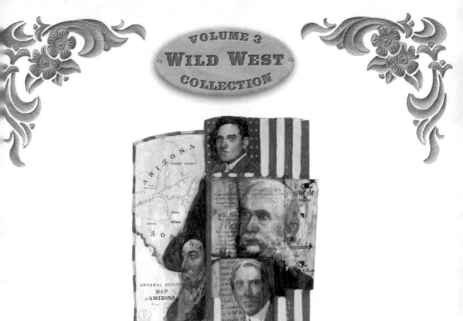

THEY LEFT THEIR MARK
Heroes and Rogues of Arizona History

Indians, scouts, ranchers, and mountain men are vividly remembered here in 16 true stories of Western adventure. Before Arizona Territory was ever surveyed, mapped, or named, its serrated mountains, savage deserts, and extreme temperatures demanded much of those first peoples who already knew it and those newcomers who were driven to explore it.

Generations passed into memory. Yet even as more settlers and opportunists came to the Southwest, the land resisted their efforts to tame it, remaining fiercely rugged from horizon to horizon.

Those whose names are recalled in these accounts were individualists who left their unique stamp — whether good or bad — forever on Arizona's history:

Alchesay, the Apache who faced monumental changes to successfully lead his people in war and in peace;

Dr. Goodfellow, the Tombstone surgeon whose bloody field experiences made him a national expert on bullet wounds;

James Addison Reavis, the swindler who almost became a Spanish baron with his own Arizona kingdom; and many more. Through their lives, experience those early days of struggle and discovery.

Softcover. 144 pages. Black and white historical photographs.
#ATMP7 $7.95

The Law of the Gun

Recounting the colorful lives and careers of gunfighters, lawmen, and outlaws, historian and author Marshall Trimble examines the mystique of the Old West and the role that guns have played in that fascination.

Tools of survival as well as deadly weapons, guns on the American frontier came to symbolize the guts and independence that people idealized in their Western heroes — even when those "heroes" were cold-blooded killers.

With the deft touch of a master storyteller, Trimble recounts the macabre humor of digging up one dead gunslinger to deliver his last shot of whiskey, the intensity of the Arizona Rangers who faced death down a gun barrel every time they pursued a crook, and the vengeful aftermath of Wyatt Earp's showdown in Tombstone. Each gripping tale will make you want to read more of how guns determined life in the West.

Softcover. 192 pages. Black and white historical photographs.
#AGNP7 $8.95

TOMBSTONE CHRONICLES
Tough Folks, Wild Times

Ed Schieffelin's hunger for the thrill of discovery survived brutal terrain and warring Apaches. When he at last struck silver in the middle of nowhere, thousands flocked to a rough mining camp that would become . . . Tombstone.

Rubbing shoulders with Clanton, Earp, and Holliday, ordinary people lived real life in extraordinary times as Tombstone became an oasis of decadence, cosmopolitan culture, and reckless violence.

Johnny Ringo was "King of the Cowboys," until he turned up dead quite mysteriously. Curly Bill Brocius, a bully with a sense of rhythm, set folks dancing . . . at gunpoint. Reverend Peabody landed some punches for the gospel. Theirs are some of 17 true stories from an Old West where anything could happen — and too often did.

Softcover. 144 pages. Black and white historical photographs.
#AWTP8 $7.95

To order these books or to request a catalog, contact:
Arizona Highways, 2039 West Lewis Avenue, Phoenix, AZ 85009-2893.
Or send a fax to 602-254-4505. Or call toll-free nationwide 1-800-543-5432.
(In the Phoenix area or outside the U.S., call 602-258-1000.)
Visit us at www.arizonahighways.com to order online.

STALWART WOMEN
Frontier Stories of Indomitable Spirit

Tough enough to walk barefoot through miles of desert and cactus forest. Strong enough to fell a man with a jaw-crunching blow. Wily enough to con the U.S. Army.

Even if you know all of the buffalo hunters, lawmen, rustlers, and warriors, you've missed the Old West's full excitement until you meet the unique women who plunged into the harsh unknown — mad Mollie Monroe on her quest for revenge, Sarah Bowman and her gigantic strength, daring Pauline Cushman behind the lines as a spy.

Life was a struggle under extremes sometimes hard to imagine. Yet these are not fictionalized stories, but the gripping reality of tough women out West. They fought for a place in the hostile wilderness, charmed their way through war zones, and commandeered arduous rescue missions. These survivors didn't buckle when disaster struck, and disaster struck often.

For danger and adventure, read these 15 gritty accounts by Tucson author Leo W. Banks. Start in the middle or read them all straight through, you'll find that each chapter stands alone as a riveting portrait of gutsy endurance.

Softcover. 144 pages. Black and white historical photographs. **#AWWP8 $7.95**

ARIZONA
HIGHWAYS
B O O K S

To order these books or to request a catalog, contact:
Arizona Highways, 2039 West Lewis Avenue, Phoenix, AZ 85009-2893.
Or send a fax to 602-254-4505. Or call toll-free nationwide 1-800-543-5432.
(In the Phoenix area or outside the U.S., call 602-258-1000.)
Visit us at www.arizonahighways.com to order online.

INTO THE UNKNOWN
Adventure on the Spanish Colonial Frontier

Centuries before Wyatt Earp and Billy the Kid rode onto the scene, Spanish-speaking pioneers and gunslingers roamed regions including what now is the American West. They didn't pretend to be saints. They gambled and swore, shot up their friends, and had tempestuous affairs. Going where no non-Indian had gone before, they lived and died in a wild new world, lured — even driven — by the power and appeal of the unknown.

It was a time of unmatchable heroism and unimaginable tragedy, set in uncharted territory that would someday become Kansas, Oklahoma, Texas, Nebraska, New Mexico, Arizona, California, Oregon, Washington, Utah, British Columbia, Colorado, Alaska.

A castaway-turned-slave becomes the West's first loner, first fugitive, and first tragic hero — all before 1540. An English pirate tries to steal California. A German lands in the Inquisition's snares. Outlaws die in a ring of fire. A sailor walks from the Pacific Northwest to Chihuahua. Unbelievable, even outrageous, but all true, these tales of courage, mayhem, and disaster by award-winning history writer Susan Hazen-Hammond take lovers of the Wild West into a vast unknown and put them in touch with a passionate, powerful past that has been neglected too long.

Softcover. 144 pages. Illustrated. **#ASCS9 $7.95**

Coming in October 1999

GRAND CANYON STORIES: THEN & NOW

Ancient path of Indian legend and destination for modern adventure, the Grand Canyon runs through human history with force and allure. Few remain unimpressed, but not everyone is content to stand on the edge in awe. This collection tells the vivid stories — past and present — of pioneering explorers, hardy idealists, extreme adventurers, and visionary individualists who have ventured into the Canyon's depths. Some returned. Some have stayed. And a few were never seen again.

In the 130 years since John Wesley Powell first navigated the rampaging Colorado River through the Grand Canyon, countless adventurous souls have followed the Canyon's beckoning. Now, in stories spanning two centuries, historian Leo Banks delves into the characters of legendary tale and historic fact, while writer/naturalist Craig Childs profiles distinctive people of today who have fashioned their lives around the West's most recognizable natural wonder.

Softcover. 192 pages, with 62 black and white photographs, including an historical portfolio and 16 contemporary portraits. **#AGCS9 $10.95**

Coming in September 1999

To order these books or to request a catalog, contact:
Arizona Highways, 2039 West Lewis Avenue, Phoenix, AZ 85009-2893.
Or send a fax to 602-254-4505. Or call toll-free nationwide 1-800-543-5432.
(In the Phoenix area or outside the U.S., call 602-258-1000.)
Visit us at www.arizonahighways.com to order online.